THE OLD WISE WOMAN

A C.G. JUNG FOUNDATION BOOK

The C. G. Jung Foundation for Analytical Psychology is dedicated to helping men and women grow in conscious awareness of the psychological realities in themselves and society, find healing and meaning in their lives and greater depth in their relationships, and live in response to their discovered sense of purpose. It welcomes the public to attend its lectures, seminars, films, symposia, and workshops and offers a wide selection of books for sale through its bookstore. The Foundation also publishes *Quadrant*, a semiannual journal, and books on Analytical Psychology and related subjects. For information about Foundation programs or membership, please write to the C. G. Jung Foundation, 28 East 39th Street, New York, NY 10016.

THE OLD WISE WOMAN

A Study of Active Imagination

RIX WEAVER

Introduction by C. A. Meier

SHAMBHALA
Boston & London
1991

SHAMBHALA PUBLICATIONS, INC.
Horticultural Hall
300 Massachusetts Avenue
Boston, Massachusetts 02115

SHAMBHALA PUBLICATIONS, INC.
Random Century House
20 Vauxhall Bridge Road
London SW1V 2SA

9 8 7 6 5 4 3 2 1
First Shambhala Edition
Printed in the United States of America on acid-free paper
Distributed in the United States by Random House, Inc., in
Canada by Random House of Canada Ltd, and in the United
Kingdom by the Random Century Group

LIBRARY OF CONGRESS CATALOGING-IN-PUBLICATION DATA
Weaver, Rix, 1902-
     The old wise woman: a study of active imagination/Rix Weaver;
introduction by C. A. Meier.—1st Shambhala ed.
        p. cm.
     Reprint. Originally published: New York : Published by Putnam for
the C. G. Jung Foundation for Analytical Psychology, 1973.
     Includes bibliographical references.
     ISBN 0-87773-605-7 (alk. paper)
     1. Imagination.   2. Psychoanalysis.   3. Jung, C. G. (Carl Gustav),
1875–1961.   I. Title.
[BF408.W355   1991]   90-53386
153.3—dc20   CIP

To my friend
MARIAN REITH
recalling talks and walks
and the Zürich scene

Acknowledgments

This volume has required a great deal of time on research—a great deal more for the Alchemical substances to be transmuted. It is an exciting but lonely occupation to do such work, for those who could help have the wisdom to leave one alone with it. I am always grateful to the people under whom I worked in Zürich, to Professor C. A. Meier and Dr. Liliane Frey-Rohn for their understanding help, to Dr. Marie-Louise von Franz, not only for her brilliant and inspiring lectures at the C. G. Jung Institute, but for her personal encouragement. To Miss Barbara Hannah I owe a great deal for her inspiring lectures on Active Imagination. To Miss Mary Nunn I say "thank you" for valuable suggestions, also to Professor A. Edwards, of the University of Western Australia, and Miss Una Thomas, of Zürich, for reading the manuscript and making many helpful suggestions, to Dr. James Kirsch, of Los Angeles, for his untiring interest. Appreciation to Dr. E. A. Bennet for reading the manuscript as it emerged crumple-winged from the chrysalis, and Lorelei Bradshaw for tireless sorting and typing, and to those people who permitted me to use their fantasy material for this book.

I also wish to express my sincere gratitude to the following authors for permission to quote from their works: Dr. Esther Harding (*Woman's Mysteries*), Dr. John Layard (*The Incest Taboo* and *The Virgin Archetype*) and Dr. James Kirsch (*Journey to the Moon* and *The Enigma of Moby Dick*).

Finally I record my indebtedness to the following publishers: Messrs. Routledge & Kegan Paul and The Bollingen Foundation for permission to quote from *The Secret of the Golden Flower* (Jung and Wilhelm), *An Introduction to the Science of Mythology* (Jung and Kerenyi), *The Mythology of the Soul* (Baynes), *The Great Mother* (Neumann), and the following works of C. G. Jung, *Mysterium Coniunctionis, Answer to Job, Psychology and Alchemy, Psychology and Religion, Aion, Essays on Contemporary Events, Spirit and Nature, Contributions to Analytical Psychology, Psychological Types* and *The Practice of Psychotherapy*: Messrs. Barrie & Rockliff for permission to quote *C. G. Jung* (E. A. Bennet) and Messrs. Ernest Benn Ltd. for permission to quote from *The Lost Language of Symbolism* (Harold Bayley).

RIX WEAVER

Contents

Introduction

IT IS a pleasure to write a few introductory words to Mrs. Rix Weaver's unique book, THE OLD WISE WOMAN.

C. G. Jung himself dealt with material arising from the "method" of Active Imagination is his private seminars, and in his Memoirs.[1]

The time has come, it seems to me, for a wider circle of interested people to be given a firsthand report of a subject which plays such an important part in the practice of Analytical Psychotherapy. This book therefore offers the opportunity to witness the development and unfolding of such a process.

Mrs. Weaver's presentation of her material is accompanied by a brilliant and comprehensive commentary that makes it easy for the reader to understand the nature and the importance of the method. Perhaps indeed the commentary makes everything seem just a little too easy. The reader should be warned that for the subject or patient the material, so admirably presented, meant a lot of "toil, sweat and tears" and could not have been undertaken and brought to a happy conclusion without tremendous effort, sacrifice and courage. It is also important to emphasize the contribution of the analyst. Nobody should attempt anything of this nature without the help and direction of an experienced "guru"— in the first place because "the perils of the soul" are considerable, in the second place because it is essential to trace the mythological parallels to what we may call the "personal myth" of the subject, in this way linking him to humanity in general and enabling him to escape the danger of getting lost in his "personal myth."

This has been achieved most convincingly by the author, and a careful reader will recognize that in handling the subject of her study, Mrs. Weaver supplies and emphasizes the support and help we have just been describing as essential.

Prof. Dr. med. C. A. Meier
Spezialarzt für Psychiatrie FMH
(Zürich)

[1] Jung, C. G. *Memories, Dreams, Reflections.* New York: Pantheon Books, Inc., 1963.

THE OLD WISE WOMAN

CHAPTER 1

Some Aspects of the Technique
of Active Imagination

WHEN one attempts to write on the subject of Active Imagination, one is immediately confronted with the question of how important is this procedure in psychotherapy. It is quite true that psychotherapy does not necessarily have to incorporate this technique. I have learned, however, that it holds a place of eminence for those patients who can successfully use it.

Psychotherapy itself is the treatment of the soul, for the soul is the birthplace or mother place of all human behavior.[1] It is true that Active Imagination enters the fields of the arts, yet itself is not valuable for its artistic quality, but for its symbolism, which, taken into account with the conscious situation, gives deeper and wider meaning to life.

A person brings a personal problem into analysis, but he brings a complete soul along with it and also his world. So though the technique crosses the boundaries of the arts, it does so because art also springs from the soul, and the more symbolic the art, the more meaningful. Both the world and the soul are supra-personal, so, except in the case of a seemingly very personal difficulty, psychotherapy crosses the boundaries of the individual to his connection with the supra-personal. Every individual is a piece of the world and carries the non-personal within himself.

The human psyche has a projecting mechanism. It is a mechanism which uses consciousness. Quite frequently the projection

[1] N.B. This word *soul* is used in its psychological sense (i.e., *psyche* from the Greek means soul), not in a religious connotation.

1

does not exactly fit the objective fact, so that analytically one is then concerned with discovering how much of the projection is colored from subjective experience. To withdraw the planks of projection could leave the ego at a great loss if it were not for the amazing thing that, from the depth of the unconscious, there will arise a new center superior to the ego. This is perhaps difficult to realize without personal experience, but I hope to make it clear in the following pages. Although Active Imagination can help a little in personal analysis, that is, with difficulties to do with the personal unconscious, I will show that its great achievement is in the realm of the non-personal depth analysis.

One of Jung's discoveries was the autonomous creative activity of the unconscious, an activity which revealed itself as having what might be termed a myth-forming propensity. He then found that this tendency could be used analytically, and he named the process Active Imagination. Why he named it Active Imagination was to differentiate it from passive imagination, and the difference will become clear in the following pages.

This particular work is an attempt to show what Active Imagination is, how it can be amplified and made meaningful for the person following this method of analysis. I have to assume that the reader is familiar with analytical procedures in order that this less familiar way may be of interest. This is in no way a case history, for at this point I am not concerned with any individual but with the process, and I want to show how the work done by a patient can be amplified by analogy, and how, in fact, we see in such work the deep roots of consciousness, and how they stretch back to bring up again symbols and ideas that have been with man from time immemorial.

Active Imagination at once includes visions, painting, modeling, writing, dancing, in fact any form which can serve the individual as a suitable channel for expression. Whatever medium or media of expression are chosen, the messages of the unconscious can become evident. By themselves, expressions of the unconscious might seem meaningless, but can become of great importance through amplification by analogy.

It is this latter aspect which is mainly my theme. However, before getting involved in an actual piece of Active Imagination and discussion of analogous material, it may be helpful to those not well acquainted with this process to say something more specific about it.

"Active Imagination" is a term which can give an impression of something elusive, so I would like to say first that there is a great deal of difference between Active Imagination and idle fantasy. Fantasy, because it does not lead into actions in the world of objective reality, can actually lead an individual away from reality, for such fantasies can be more fascinating and less demanding than the outer world. Active Imagination is, as I hope to show later, fantasy with a difference, fantasy in fact, which has the full co-operation of the participating ego.

The history of the method is briefly this. Freud, in his work with the unconscious psyche, discovered that the mind will, by association of ideas, bring together material of significance. He developed his discovery into the method of "free association." Using free association, a patient expresses freely what comes into his mind, one idea touching off another. Freud found such a way to lead to hidden complexes.[2] Jung found this method very productive, and he also saw behind the material thus contacted a hidden continuum. The inclusion of ego attention in the picture established a connecting line, so it was not only the fact that complexes were revealed, which was important, but Jung questioned further what the unconscious was attempting to reveal via the complexes. Now in analyzing dreams, Jung would ask for the patient's associations to the dream content, the dream content always remaining the center, and each association relating back to it. This, however, is not to be confused with Active Imagination. In the latter, spontaneous eruptions from the unconscious are woven together, not only thereby revealing complexes, but also the unconscious effort to reveal continuity and meaning, and by way of the particular material itself, a means of understanding and dealing with it. So it can be said, in short, that free associa-

[2] N.B. Quite independently of Freud, before the two great discoverers met, Jung, through his use of the Word Association Test, discovered difficulties with persons on whom the test was used, such as breaks in the continuity of conscious thought, eruptions into consciousness of ideas set off by the stimulus word. It was seen that such responses were attached to the stimulus word by an emotional tone. These strange breaks led Jung to his theory of complexes. This idea and the word "complex" passed into common usage in psychology.

tion leads to the discovery of complexes, whereas Active Imagination leads beyond to the structure of the psyche, in which psychic life is contained and maintained. That is, it not only exposes and explains personal properties of the psyche, but it leads into and reveals the non-personal realm. It is this non-personal realm which is the source of myths, fairy tales and specific forms of religious belief and rituals. It is here one finds the basic struggles of mankind, the psychic growth and the forms upon which consciousness rests.

An analysis of the personal contents of the psyche precedes, as a rule, the effective use of Active Imagination. In general, it is a medium used by people who have made considerable progress in analysis. Patients in the earlier stages of analytical treatment are concerned mainly with personal factors. In fact, it is not a method that is suitable to all people and cannot be used indiscriminately, for it leads inevitably beyond the conscious mind to the very basis of psychic life, to the inner world of nature, to darkness and to the roots of ethical and cultural development.

It might be asked when it is suitable to use Active Imagination, and I can only say that is something that cannot be decided arbitrarily. Suppose, for instance, that, in an advanced stage of analysis, figures arise in dreams or visions and it is realized these are figures appearing to have meaning but which one's conscious knowledge cannot yet appreciate. The question then is how does one know whether they do have such meaningfulness and how does one discover their meanings? Now if one holds such figures in the mind in a contemplative way, that is, just regarding them as if one's ego is the onlooker although involved—and this is much more difficult to do than it appears, for the ego wants, as a rule, to take precedence—it is as if imagination begins to stir and a dream of the unconscious begins to unfold. Generally the ego is included in the drama, moving through the scene or asking questions. So with an attitude that acknowledges the reality of the psyche, a conversation begins between conscious and unconscious, and thus one enters the dialectic method that allows the psyche freedom of expression. Ego consciousness then, disposed to genuine inquiry, is like a torchlight thrown onto the unconscious, and the correct approach brings corresponding and often remarkable co-operation from the psychic hinterland.

Dialectic used in Active Imagination is not merely chatting with oneself. Common experience makes familiar to all of us the situation in which we find ourselves trying to put into action some carefully thought-out plan, only to find that some counter-decision is worrying us so that we cannot act freely. Therefore we have to think through these two opposing sides of the question. We then realize that it is not only our conscious mind which is concerned in the matter, but that there is an "otherness" operating as well. The struggle between the two contending forces can even become a dialectic until a clear decision is arrived at. We still do not know who or what this "other" is; all we know is that we are forced thereby to be more thorough. In Active Imagination, we first recognize the "otherness" of the psyche, then enter into the situation prepared to learn what has to be said from the other side. The process is very different from thinking the thing out. What is actually done is to let something happen in the psyche quite freely, while the ego participates not as director, but as the actively experiencing one.

So one could say the gateway for Active Imagination springs open when a person in analysis is ready for this means of expression. There are times when no amount of rational thinking can help us portray what we are trying to express, so we turn to brush or pen or music in an attempt to say what seems unsayable. I'll give you a simple illustration. I had a patient who had had a recurring dream since childhood. She was sent to me after quite some time of analysis with someone else, and one day she told me about the dream: "I was in a long passage with three doors on either side and a seventh door at the farthest end. Each time I attempted to pass down this hallway, a dark presence like a cloud descended and forced me back." We interpreted that dream in several ways, but we were obviously missing something vitally important, and the unconscious insisted that it should be understood. That is a thing most interesting about the unconscious, if one fails to arrive at its significance it comes up again with greater force and sometimes changes its mode of expression until understood. Now this seemed a time to start Active Imagination. The unconscious obviously had something important to say, for not only the problem but the healing means are in the patient. So the patient was encouraged to sit and get into the mood of the dream and feel herself in the situation of the dream picture. She told me this was extremely frightening, for when she saw again the dark cloud, she wanted to turn away from the task. However, she was able to fight the "presence" and gradually pass through each door in turn. Each of the rooms she entered presented her with an amazing picture that could be related to her own problems, but they also pointed to something beyond the personal which would take time for us to understand. A most interesting thing, however, was the fact that, after facing the experiences of the six rooms, she was able to go through the seventh door at the far end of the hall. This is the part of the Active Imagination I would like to dwell on briefly. Beyond the seventh door, she met a man with a book fastened open across his forehead. This, he told her, was a book of rules. The rules she had laid down for herself were numerous and powerful, and through this figure, she discovered an animus figure who, with some women, is an arbitrary dictator. The animus is the masculine aspect of a woman's unconscious psyche. This animus had had a tremendous power in her life, restricting and crippling her attempts to live. In Active Imagination, she conversed with him and persuaded him to remove the book of rules. Now the animus, once it is confronted by the ego, proves through his progressive education to be friend and not foe. The animus functions as a discriminator, but too much discrimination directed at everything a woman wants to do means her own feminine thoughts and feelings are swamped. When she assesses other people and outer situations, it can be with such criticism that she cannot enter into life. Once she begins to discriminate between the dictation of the animus and her own genuine feelings, she becomes more whole. So it was not surprising that, when the patient met this figure and asked him to remove the book from his forehead, he entered into her work in a positive way and went with her in search of the hidden treasure, namely the unknown self.[3]

This illustrates one of the many ways in analysis in which the method provides new ground and deeper insight. To have told this patient she had an arbitrary animus would not have helped. In fact he would take over her attitude and possibly argue the

[3] A portion of the Active Imagination she did is to be found, with interpretation, on page 135.

issue, but when he reveals himself in such a way to an unsuspecting ego, the situation becomes convincing.

As everyone knows, there are people who feel a capacity within themselves, but have absolutely no means of using it. They feel restricted and often give up any attempt toward an outlet. Many people with such a restriction find compensation in fantasy life. Idle fantasy occupies them without its adding anything to their development. It has been my experience that where there is no outlet, if once the imagination is stirred by conscious intervention, the person begins to develop, and where there is a compensating overdevelopment of idle fantasy, just a little Active Imagination will help the person pursue a more definite course and a more constructive one.

Within the personality, embedded in the unconscious, are complexes living a life of their own like separate egos. Normal man depends on his complexes for much of his inspiration. The complexes have a positive role, but also a negative one, for they give rise to inner feelings of uncertainty, they can have a disintegrating effect on consciousness. Analysis of the personal unconscious reveals much of this unconscious material. Archetypes are not so readily brought into consciousness. They are often vague and borderline. We might find a "nay" countering our conscious "yea" and we are led to ask who this other fellow is. By listening as if it were an ego speaking, we can hear what he has to say. In this way we can contact such figures as the animus and anima. The animus is the unconscious masculinity in the feminine psyche, while the anima represents the unconscious feminine in the masculine psyche. The personifying of such archetypes makes it possible to have a discussion with them without the ego having been swamped by them in a way in which they are indistinguishable from one's own thoughts or moods. To personify such figures means to acknowledge their entity. For instance, a man might be suffering from a mood. He feels the mood as himself. He might be so blinded by the mood that he does not see it as unreasonable, or he might even have a vague knowledge that the mood does not have to do with his masculine ego. He might even be conscious enough to say or think "I know the mood is unreasonable, but I can't stop being like this." If he personifies that mood, say as the anima, for she frequently acts moodily, he has a chance to disentangle himself from the mood and look at it objectively. To be identical with the mood means to be in a primitive state of possession wherein the ego is submerged by primitive emotion and not in a position to reason. To reason is an attribute of man's conscious logos, so by separating from the unconscious by means of personification, one is no longer identified with it and gains the possibility of critical judgment. A situation is created wherein one can stand back and look at things squarely.

The idea of personifying the figures or moods of the unconscious may seem very strange. A person who has experienced a moment of talking to himself, trying to convince himself perhaps of something, will realize there is a spontaneous inclination in some people to do this. To carry out in Active Imagination such a separating process means the ego frees itself from contamination. Thus separating and objectifying the unconscious is essentially a process of maturity.

To seek the meaning of something revealed by Active Imagination does not mean that it has to be analyzed as dreams are analyzed. Active Imagination is different from dreams, for the latter come unbidden and the ego has no say in the matter, while Active Imagination is the direct response of the unconscious to consciousness or ego participation. When the ego is thus involved, it means naturally that the images are half consciously chosen, and this brings the streams of conscious and unconscious together. The participant is asking questions and the unconscious is giving the other side of the picture. As will readily be seen, we are responsible for Active Imagination in a way in which we are not so directly responsible for dreams. The former can have an ethical value not always seen in a dream. The dream tells of how things are, while Active Imagination brings in a forward movement and attempts some level of achievement. Now there is another important point I think necessary to mention.

Experience has shown that the figures of the unconscious, personified in the ways indicated, are living and numinous. Archetypal figures are contacted and these figures can have a powerful effect. Say one discovers, for instance, a wise old man or wise old woman whose utterances are meaningful and, as the name suggests, extremely wise, wiser by far than the participating ego. Such figures are archetypal and collective, and they speak with the age-old wisdom of the world. The effect produced on the ego is to be so inspired by them that the ego accepts them as personal and can become inflated, or, put another way, the participant can identify his ego with the wise old man. Such a thing is natural and here the analytical process is to keep the separation. The necessity for this will become clear when we consider that not only superior things are revealed, but also the dark forces of nature, the chaotic, even demonic, aspects. It is possible also to have a negative inflation, for if one did not keep the separation, one could be crushed as well as inspired by archetypal material. Therefore, what the participant is in life is important, so also is the necessity for a good ego development. No one is personally responsible for such archetypal images, but one is responsible for the discovery of the meaning they have for one, individually. Only by recognition and transformation can powers of the unconscious become positive qualities of one's psychic life. It is not a matter of knowing only the acceptable aspects of nature, but also qualities inacceptable to the standards of the participating ego.

I had occasion to analyze a man and his wife who had both undergone a previous analysis for some years. This earlier analysis was non-Jungian but obviously some terms were used which should be used only with great discretion. These people had both been told the wife had a powerful unconscious, that she was a witch exercising a tremendously powerful effect on the husband. She consequently thought of herself as *the witch* and her husband believed that she, as "witch," was responsible for his own grave difficulties. They had both gone into an inflation. I had extraordinary difficulty in getting her down to size. While there was something of truth in the claim, she had to see she was not the witch archetype itself. She was an ordinary human being and not a goddess or a demonic power, while he had to become responsible toward his own anima. So great was the inflation that they felt I was robbing them of vital meaning. Both these people had been born Catholics but both had neglected the Church because it was no longer meaningful for them. Now the archetype of God carries the most tremendous energy. The Church as carrier of the symbol of God no longer worked for them, therefore the energy fell back into the unconscious and the powerful qualities previously ascribed to God now were applied to the wife. When they heard the word "witch" they grasped at that as if everything was now understood, and she became deluded by an idea of super-human power.

Jung says: "Did not Nietzsche predict that God was dead, and that the Superman would be heir to the divine inheritance; that fatal ropedancer and fool? It is an immutable psychological law that a projection which has come to an end always returns to its origin. So when somebody hits upon the singular idea that God is dead, or does not exist at all, the psychic image of God, which represents a definite dynamic and psychic structure, finds its way back to the subject and produces a condition in which the thinker believes himself to be 'like God'; in other words, it brings out all the qualities which are only characteristic of fools and madmen and therefore lead to a castastrophe." [4]

In such a situation, it is necessary to establish a new center, which is the tendency of the psyche, that meaningfulness may be established.

A more simple case of a person being in the hands of his shadow and subsequently becoming conscious of it is the following illustration. This case was one where actual Active Imagination was not done, but something which can illustrate how things can go along these lines even in the initial stages of analysis. This particular man was the black sheep of the family, really living out the shadow of all of them. He came to me one Saturday afternoon and asked me to lock him up because the betting shops were open. I had other people to see, so I put him into a room by himself and gave him some clay to occupy him. He modeled a figure that showed with extreme clarity the weaknesses of his personality. A bulky human form having neither hands nor feet suggested the obstacle in his way. Without hands and feet, there was an inadequate capacity to cope with life; it pointed to a condition which could only be overcome by the easy way out, that of embezzler. He had had, up to then, a few sessions of analysis. When he had studied the form he modeled, saw it outside, where he could look at it objectively as if it were a separate factor, it proved much more helpful to him than any attempt to recognize

[4] C. G. Jung, *Essays on Contemporary Events*, pages 69-70.

his shadow. He was perfectly aware of his anti-social deeds, he was their victim, and helpless. He had come to accept himself as a bad lot, and here at last he was able to distinguish between the ego, which really was struggling for something better, and the enemy, which overpowered him. In this way, he was in a better position to cope with his irresistible impulses toward anti-social deeds. In fact, he was both horrified and amazed at having produced such a speaking piece of work while he fumbled with clay in hours when he had literally to hide from temptation. He was not interested, at this stage, in the collective shadow or archetypal material, for his effort was to save himself. And this is the correct attitude. It is only later that one learns that the individual effort has meaning beyond oneself.

The whole process of Active Imagination is one demanding responsibility, for whether for good or evil, active fantasying affects both the character and life. In fact, Active Imagination becomes true or, to phrase it differently, one could say that, in a symbolic way, it is the germ material of later life, in much the same way as ideas precede efforts that bring them into existence.[5] Therefore, it determines one's truth and precedes what one is, that is, it is the stuff from which one's world is created. This is a tremendously big thing, for it brings the flow of unrealized events into existence, thereby advancing the process of individuation, that is, the more meaningful and fuller life leading to wholeness of being.

The greater understanding which Active Imagination affords the participant provides him with a basis for the problem of life. A knowledge of archetypal influences provides meaning and indeed, in a certain sense, security. In our day, individuality is stressed, but that is not individuation. Individuality can be conscious, while individuation goes beyond. That is, the process of individuation establishes a connection between the ego and the self.[6] This, I think, will be much clearer when I give an illustra-

[5] N.B. Consciousness for Jung is wrested from the unconscious, so the widening effect this work has on consciousness naturally affects one's character and life.

[6] N.B. The self as a Jungian concept is explained in the Glossary, and a fuller discussion of the meaning of the term can be read in Jung's *Psychological Types*.

tion of a whole series of Active Imagination with its analogical material. Sufficient now to say that the finding of ourselves is both a reductive and a synthetic process. Analysis of the personal unconscious which precedes depth analysis should also be synthetic as well as reductive. Merely to reduce is to pull away every foundation on which the ego has established itself, a foundation which has been necessary to meet the demands of life, for the ego personality is established according to the "funds on hand." The synthetic process builds toward something, that is, for each plank that has to be removed, being either warped or white-ant ridden, there must be a healthy plank ready to insert, so that the whole structure does not collapse. It is true one has to face the other side of the personality, that is, the shadow of the ego or persona. What one is, is established. This other side is not merely a caricature; it has an important function, and not only its negativity has to be learned, but its potential. First to accept the shadow takes all one's courage and strength, in fact a very great love. Can one love one's dark side enough to redeem it? People in analysis are making that attempt every day. For people who have cherished a resplendent ego, it can mean a great deal of humility, but at the same time a more developed personality results. On the other hand, the person who has lived beneath his level will appreciate the gold of his character which for him has been concealed. The accepting of the gold of the personality is often a greater problem than the acceptance of humiliating truths, for the realization of one's potential for creative activity carries with it an obligation to realize those potentialities to the full. Living below what one can really be is really an escape from life. When I speak of creative activity in this sense, I mean that life in every way is creative experience. To live life fully, whatever the sphere of one's capacities, is an art, and a creative art.

Now the shadow is often thought to contain only the dark aspects of the personality, but if one thinks of the shadow as an unlived part of the personality, it will readily be seen that it can contain both good and bad. The shadow is mainly unconscious, and unconscious properties have the disquieting effect of revealing themselves in outer acts. Because they are unlived, not integrated into one's way of life, they are primitive. Primitive emotions frighten us, so that we are rather inclined to cut off the shadow regardless of its good potential. To know this side of oneself means, then, one is in a position to choose, and choice carries responsibility. To realize such opposites in oneself needs courage and work on oneself. Then when choice is conscious, one is not merely being acted upon by a compelling force, but one becomes responsible in an entirely new way. All one's animal cages have to be tended, and people often fight shy of consciousness as if they already knew the demands of such responsibility. However, it is only by consciousness that we can live by consent rather than by compensation.

In this regard, I would like to tell of a man who came to me for analysis. Like the previous case quoted, the person's difficulties concerned at this stage a personal shadow problem. He had been sent to me from another analyst and I found him to be very rational. He knew how things should be, and was puzzled that in spite of what he knew, things did not work out well. He had a difficult marriage; his wife had turned against him, not even allowing him to sleep in his own home. He constantly tried to do what he considered to be the right things, therefore he read books on marriage and attempted to solve the problem via his intellect. It was obvious the man was out of touch with his Eros nature, that is, feeling values and a sense of what constitutes real relationship were foreign to him. One could say he was trying to be right without the whole of his nature supporting him. It was absolutely no good saying anything more which his intellect could swallow. A dream, however, gave the necessary impetus for him to touch on the anima problem. He dreamed: "I see my dead uncle who speaks to me. I know he is dead and wonder at it. He laughs and says it can be so, and as he leaves, he calls advice about solving the problem. I do not recall what the advice was, but found myself moving a coffin in which I knew there was a dead woman."

I suggested the uncle could represent a dead part of his masculinity, for among other things, he was impotent. By discussing the possibility of who the dead woman could be, we arrived at the idea she could be a feminine part of him, indeed his anima or soul, and with her dead, it meant that relating to his wife and even to life became a very difficult thing to do.

He decided to give the matter some thought. Since it was only a dream it seemed to him that to spend time on it was ridiculous, yet that I regarded it as important impressed him. He was not asked to do Active Imagination, because he was not at an advanced stage of analysis. However, next time he came, he said that in contemplating this dream, he had the very vivid impression that he had lifted the lid of the coffin and rubbed the woman's hands. He added that he was sure it meant nothing and both dream and impression were quite a bit silly. The following session, he brought the news that the woman had sat up, and to his surprise the coffin had crumbled to ashes. He was most impressed by the fact that something which he had *merely imagined* held in itself an element of surprise for him and also that it seemed to move of its own accord. He was experiencing the autonomy of the unconscious, a matter which is always profoundly moving when the attitude of the participant has been overrational.

Then came a period in which he said he felt afraid of the darkness of night; it was as if an uncanny presence pervaded the house where he dwelt alone. He was sure he had never been afraid before. He discovered this figure of the unconscious was so living that it seemed uncanny to him. In fact, it all felt spooky, but after discussing the phenomenon later, he said: "I've had a strange experience. This woman walked by my side and held my hand. She said she was grateful that I had saved her life. I pointed out it was not I, and that I had no power to restore life, but she assured me I had done a most important thing when I had lifted the lid and rubbed her hands. The most remarkable thing is that she called me by my Christian name and it sent tingles all through me. It was indeed very real and thrilling even though my conscious mind knows it was a fantasy. It did have its own reality, and I know I was not experiencing spooks."

He realized the feminine figure had life in the unconscious and was connected in a vital way within him. From then on, his endeavor became more feeling-toned rather than being intellectual decisions. He began to show feeling where he had shown none before. The old pattern commenced to fade away. Then came, of course, the animus problem of the wife, who then went to a clinic. I quote this case to show that it can be such a small amount of work as this, which allowed him consciously to carry forward the message of the dream, that has magical effect. Of course the whole problem was not by that overcome, and I do not know what happened, as he moved away. This man came naturally to the place where he did an Active Imagination without being told anything about such a process. If it happens naturally, one accepts it. Actually, it sometimes happens that a patient comes to analysis because of irrational fantasies that do not fit his rational attitude, and so he feels something is wrong. The analyst accepts the fantasy, and this acceptance is the first therapeutic step. Something in the patient is given value and he feels less afraid, is less over-powered and gradually emerges out of the frightening sea of the unconscious. That is, he gets a stronger ego standpoint, which is able to deal with the unconscious.

There is sometimes confusion in classifying Active Imagination. Everyone knows that it is possible to fantasy in a passive way, and one recognizes these fantasies which seem to happen of their own accord. Now when one steps in and consciously takes part in the fantasy or theme of the unconscious, maintaining awareness of the ego, one has stepped into Active Imagination. Consequently, the ego has effect on what happens, bringing its own characteristics to bear upon the material. For instance, one woman contacted a feminine figure in her Active Imagination. At one point, this figure stepped into a lake where the patient knew a man was sleeping in the depths. She clung to the hair of the female figure to hold her from going into the water. She was days before she could move on in this Active Imagination, for she felt she could not let her go into the deep water. She explained it this way: "I cannot let her go because I would have to follow her and I would drown. [It was as if she felt this figure to be an insepara-ble part of herself.] It would be the end of me, for I cannot swim or dive into such depths. Yet what is going to happen to this young man?" She was right to hesitate and take heed of the restrictions the ego placed on her. She responded to this fear as she would in real life. Later, she was able to let the figure proceed with the rescue work, and find ways and means by which she could help. After days of suffering, she could let the woman go and build a fire to warm the young man when he should be brought forth from the deep waters. The conscious situation de-manded due recognition of her fears even though she was concerned at not being able to let things happen. For someone else, it may have been correct to overcome fear and take the plunge, but for her at that moment, it could have been dangerous, for her fears were very real and protective. When an analyst knows that a person is building her world in this process, he knows it is important to acknowledge and respect these fears, and it is just here he can step in with the life line. In this connection, I asked quite practically: "What would you do in life in this case? Is there not something you can do in the situation?" She replied: "Of course, I would naturally get a rug, light a fire, and get food for the man. But would it be right to be so practical here?"

The last question brings us to another point. People often think they have to be somewhat fantastic in Active Imagination, whereas according to the situation of the patient, it is often the practical solution that brings one through. This is the work the ego does, not to let the unconscious get out of hand. In this case, it was right she should light a fire. It was a matter of bringing her out of the unconscious, where she had escaped into the realm of archetypal images, into the practical world where the genius she had could develop creatively and not swamp her weak ego. She also realized this. Jung says, "Over the whole procedure, there seems to reign a dim foreknowledge, not only of the pattern but the meaning. Image and meaning are identical and as the first takes shape so the latter becomes clear." [7] It is also true that, according to the conscious situation, it is necessary to overcome inhibiting factors and have the courage to plunge into the situation to discover what the unconscious tries to say. *The ego standpoint is always important.*

There is also Active Imagination which goes, as it were, beyond the realm of the ego, where the whole process is projected. This is not to be confused with fantasies that proceed from the unconscious without intervention. They are not what is known as passive fantasying in that they come from concentration by the ego. Free rein and loving attention are given to the theme of the psyche which enable the fantasies to take form. Thus the fantasy brings forth a drama before, beyond and transcending ego. Here, the ego still suffers the impact, but at this level finds it has very little to say.

I have seen, also, a complete fairy tale take form, springing in-

[7] C. G. Jung, *Spirit and Nature*, page 414.

voluntarily from the psyche. Active Imagination was being done, yet it seemed that it was necessary for a pause to be made and a statement of the structure of the ego to be expressed. At this time, it was seen but dimly why it should be so, for it appeared like something that did not belong. Only later was it obvious that it had to be said. Taken as a statement of the ego, it was important to the progress.

To establish or state what is real Active Imagination is not easy, for it is not only the Active Imagination itself, but the Active Imagination in *relation to the level of the person doing it.* One sees sometimes grotesque fantasy that leads nowhere. Here the analyst has to know what he is doing, for in certain cases, grotesque inhuman fantasy can, in given time and circumstance, mold into something of real value. That is the possibility the analyst watches for. The dreams will have bearing on it, for dreams can actually correct a wrong process. Where Active Imagination is being done according to the need of the unconscious, I have seen dreams that support and stimulate the Active Imagination. On the other hand, a man who was playing with Active Imagination, writing entirely from his head, dreamed he had beheaded an animal.

I had a patient whose fantasy material was artistically beautiful. Evil powers were clothed with menacing yet majestic words. They were grand words aesthetically selected for effect. They led him into believing he was a Shakespeare. He was so elated by his choice that it was months before the words began to say something. They were like a smoke trail in the air. Then at the moment the ego began to suffer the impact, they became real. Although the work was being written in the first person, there was no real participation, no suffering, no feeling. The ego was merely dragged in to experience a euphoria. Here is where the danger lies and where the analyst has to hold firmly on. In this case the patient suddenly grew sick of it, so thoroughly fed up, he began to write from feeling participation. That was the beginning of real work. His life was one of this illusionary character and at the point that feeling came in, he suffered. Fantasy which merely excites and elates is not Active Imagination.

It is true that in Active Imagination one follows what comes up, yet it is always partly consciously selected. It is as if the unconscious gives the content and the conscious helps to mold the

form. One could not speak without the other. Thus one recognizes
that things written from pure ego selection have a different
quality. In Active Imagination the ego and the unconscious are
interdependent. The ego pays attention, gives warm acceptance
to the unconscious image, suffers it, feels it and co-operates in
formulating it.

There are many levels of Active Imagination, and the closer
the work is to the conscious level, the more important it is for that
particular ego *only*. At the same time with equal suffering and
participation, universally valid symbols use an ego, which is ready,
for the expression of things that are in themselves beyond ego.
That is, things that have always "been" and that have a universal
underlay of mythological and religious motifs come to the fore.

Until one has experience with Active Imagination, it is sometimes thought that if a person is writing a fantasy in the first person, he is doing Active Imagination, because then the ego is
involved. The crux of Active Imagination is in how far one is
feelingly involved or engaged in what one is writing or experiencing, putting into clay or painting. One does not directly paint
in the first person, yet a painting can be a telling piece of Active
Imagination related to the conscious and unconscious. In so far
as one is really involved, the ego is in it. The first piece of work
I have chosen for the main theme of this book falls into the
category of Active Imagination which is beyond ego. James Kirsch
has said of such a piece of work when writing of "Journey to the
Moon" that "an Auseinandersetzung takes place within the
intense concentration on the inner process. This concentration is
characterized by a keen perception of Images as well as the
thoughts which arise in her (the patient), accompanied by a
warm affectionate participation of the conscious ego." [8] In the
Journal of Analytical Psychology, 1956, Michael Fordham has
pointed out the danger of using the term Active Imagination too
loosely. It is a work that is done consciously. The ego is separated
from the flow of fantasy, thus allowing conscious participation.
I have noticed with some patients that they desire to embark on
what Dr. Fordham calls "imaginative activity" [9] until at a point

[8] J. Kirsch (1955), *Journey to the Moon, Studien zur Analytischer Psychologie* C. G. *Jung*, Vol. VI, Rascher, Zürich.

[9] Refer Fordham, article on A. I., *Journal of Analytical Psychology*, May
1956.

where they separate the ego and participate in the interplay, they begin Active Imagination. It seems in such cases important to state the ego more definitely in order that the work can proceed, much as a child does when he indulges in "imaginative activity" in order to enlarge and give value to the ego.

In summing up the position on Active Imagination, I assume the following:

1. That to pay attention to moods, to autonomous fantasy fragments, to extend the meaning of dreams by fantasy, etc., is the first move of the ego to objectify in this regard, and this objectifying is in itself the beginning of ego participation.
2. That involvement can take different forms.

   (a) The ego can initiate fantasy to find meaning of dreams, etc.

   (b) That one can find oneself caught by fantasy that forces itself into consciousness much as the dream does. In such a situation, the ego is not lost in a flight of fantasy, but watches in a way that has an objective attitude to the images. The ego is the *conscious* recorder.

I will attempt to clarify this rather difficult point. Every analyst meets the patient who has endless fantasy. I had one whose fantasies were of a paranoic nature, and he, as an ego, was taken over by them. That is, for him they were absolutely an external reality. He had no capacity as ego to say, "Who am I and what is this fantasy?" He could not separate himself from it. Such a condition is pathological and is quite different from the fantasy to which one submits and *knows* that one submits, for this conscious submission is the health of a developed ego, even when he allows things to happen without intervention. He has the capacity to stand between two worlds, and fantasy material on this level has the possibility of bringing up symbolical material far beyond the capacity of the recording ego.

   (c) That one can catch a fragment of fantasy, or *initiate* fantasy and enlarge it by participation and intervention. This would bring in a subjective attitude to the unconscious material. Being consciously involved in the material means it comes under a greater restriction from the ego.

(Often in Active Imagination both processes (b) and (c) alternate as they do with the creative artist, and this contributes to the difficulty in typing the creative personality who moves between the subjective and objective attitude. Jung's work on Poetic Art,[10] although referring to the creative artist, has tremendous bearing on the individual approach to the unconscious via Active Imagination.)

3. (a) That ego participation is in the work from the moment of objective interest.

    (b) That ego participation increases with the involvement in the drama.

    (c) That all is not Active Imagination that includes the ego as part of the recorded activity, and where the ego selects too arbitrarily or ritualistically.

4. That where the whole work is projected much as alchemical writings,[11] and mostly this is at an advanced stage of psychic maturity, it is equally Active Imagination. Here one is in a realm that influences, but remains beyond, ego participation, which can be recorded as such. As referred to in 2(b), one often discovers here the more universal and eternal symbols, myths of beginnings, immortality, etc.

5. That the most important criterion of what is Active Imagination is not so much that the activity of the ego is actually recorded in the work, but that the ego undergoes meaningful participation no matter which form of expression it takes.

6. That ego participation differs in different people. The introvert can have an objective attitude to the unconscious and the extravert a subjective attitude in this realm. Both are possible. Only the person who has done the work is the final judge of what is meaningful for him. Meaningful work is not an egotistical selection, but requires the capacity to acknowledge certainty and uncertainty at the same time.

In the following quotation, Jung expresses the art required to enter into real Active Imagination: "The art of letting things happen, action in non-action, letting go of oneself, as taught by

---

[10] Jung, *Contributions to Analytical Psychology*, pages 240ff.

[11] N.B. C. G. Jung's *Psychology of the Transference* and *Psychology and Alchemy* explain the projected images in the working out of inner psychological requirements.

Meister Eckhart, became a key to me with which I was able to open the door to the 'Way.' The key is this: We must be able to let things happen in the psyche. For us this becomes a real art of which few people know anything. Consciousness is forever interfering, helping, correcting, and negating, and never leaving the simple growth of the psychic process in peace. It would be a simple enough thing to do if only simplicity were not the most difficult of all things. It consists solely in watching objectively the development of any fragment of fantasy. Nothing could be simpler than this, and yet right here the difficulties begin. Apparently no fantasy-fragment is at hand—yes, there is one, but it is too stupid! Thousands of good excuses are brought against it: one cannot concentrate on it; it is too boring; what could come of it? It is 'nothing but,' etc. The conscious raises prolific objections; in fact, it often seems bent upon blotting out the spontaneous fantasy-activity despite the intention, nay, the firm determination of the individual to allow the psychic processes to go forward without interference. In many cases there exists a veritable spasm of the conscious.

"If one is successful in overcoming the initial difficulty, criticism is likely to start afterwards and attempt to interpret the fantasy, to classify, to aestheticize, or to depreciate it. The temptation to do this is almost irresistible. After a complete and faithful observation, free rein can be given to the impatience of the conscious; in fact it must be given, else obstructing resistances develop. But each time the fantasy material is to be produced, the activity of the conscious must be put aside.

"In most cases the results of these efforts are not very encouraging at first. It is chiefly a matter of typical fantasy material which admits of no clear statement as to whence it comes or whither it is going. Moreover, the way of getting at the fantasies is individually different. For many people it is easiest to write them; others visualize them; and others again draw and paint them with or without visualization. In cases of a high degree of inflexibility in the conscious, oftentimes the hands alone can fantasy; they model or draw figures that are quite foreign to the conscious.

"These exercises must be continued until the cramp in the conscious is released, or, in other words, until one can let things happen, which was the immediate goal of the exercise. In this way a new attitude is created, an attitude which accepts the irrational and the unbelievable simply because it is what is happening. This attitude would be poison for a person who has already been overwhelmed by things that just happen, but it is of the highest value for one who, with an exclusively conscious critique, chooses from the things that happen only those appropriate to his consciousness, and thus gets gradually drawn away from the stream of life into a stagnant backwater.

"At this point the way traveled by the two above-mentioned types seems to separate. Both have learned to accept what comes to them. (As Master Lü Tzŭ teaches: 'When occupations come to us we must accept them; when things come to us we must understand them from the ground up.') One man (extravert) will chiefly take what comes to him from without, and the other (introvert) [12] what comes from within, and, as determined by the law of life, the one will have to take from without something he never could accept from without, and the other will accept from within things which have always been excluded before.

"This reversal of one's being means an enlargement, heightening, and enrichment of the personality when the previous values are adhered to along with the change, provided, of course, they are not mere illusions. If the values are not retained, the man goes over to the other side, and passes from fitness to unfitness, from adaptedness to the lack of it, from sense to nonsense, and from reason even to mental disease. The way is not without danger. Everything good is costly, and the development of the personality is one of the most costly of all things. It is a question of yea-saying to oneself, of taking the self as the most serious of tasks, keeping conscious of everything done, and keeping it constantly before one's eyes in all its dubious aspects—truly a task that touches us to the core." [13]

[12] Insertions (extravert) and (introvert) are mine.
[13] C. G. Jung and Richard Wilhelm, *Secret of the Golden Flower*, pages 90ff.

CHAPTER 2

The Individual Nature
of Active Imagination

MY OWN experience has been, and I have seen the same thing occur for others, that when one enters into Active Imagination with real participation, one comes eventually to a situation which seems insoluble. One is *really* tested and comes up against a problem which affects one as much as difficulties in outer life. In this condition the doer suffers in a way according to his nature. He might wait patiently for some unfoldment, or await the direction of a dream, or even sweat and work and force himself. This very flow and non-flow can bring up resistance to the work, for there is always a yea-nay reaction to inner development regardless of conscious knowledge of its value, yet one has entered a drama as important as outer reality and approaches it with what one is. That final statement is important. It is what one is that provides variation in the work. If one is an intellectual conjurer it will be revealed in too much conscious direction. In Active Imagination the ego certainly has the prerogative of leadership, a fact which separates it from passive imagining, but ultimately it must come to balance of freedom for both sides. That is freedom of expression for the unconscious and interest and participation from the conscious side.

Another important point is the doer's integrity toward the unconscious and the process itself. This integrity is sometimes present in the beginning of such work and sometimes develops with involvement in the work. Where there is no integrity the work has little or no value.

As I see it, one can be too arbitrary in stating what is true Active Imagination, because the meaning for the doer is the final assessment. I knew a woman who did Active Imagination in which she produced a more stylized or conventional form of Christian image. She discovered this was the only way she could go, although she had not previously been aware of it.

This brings us to level and individual requirement. On one level of work, an image can be chosen which is right and proper at that level, but certainly not adequate at another level. For instance, a woman came to a place in Active Imagination in which a fire must burn forever. She had promised to keep alight this everlasting fire. The problem of fuel arose, and the forest, which was particularly her forest, would have to be gradually destroyed. Here was a drama, the preservation of fire or tree. Looking at such a situation in which one is not personally involved it may not seem very serious, but to the participant such a situation is difficult and tense. There are emotional and important symbolic values on either side and there seems no solution. One is up against forces and powerless, and there is nothing one can do but stew in the situation. If the choice is to cut the tree, an important symbol of life has been destroyed. If the fire is allowed to die out another symbol is affected. One can say from the intellect, why worry, for the fire revealed itself as eternal fire, so does it need this particular human help? The fact is the Active Imagination took the attitude that human help *was* needed and here it involved deep feeling values. One cannot go back and scrap what has come into the work and say, "Now if I did it this way, it would work out." The statement has been made and that is exactly what one is up against, and the doer is somewhere aware of the importance, and this awareness makes impossible anything but earnest treatment of such a situation. In this case a dream which included a little blackboy brought this figure into the Active Imagination. The unconscious moved of itself and involved him in the drama of fire and tree. It was this native boy, close to nature, who was able to tell her that the first man who had brought fire to the earth had hidden it in the stones so that it was eternally available. With this problem solved, the work could continue. Of course the writer knew that flints can produce fire. Yet the idea as presented in this connection had never occurred to her. She, in seeking a solution, had thought of many things such as oil wells. As this had not felt right she could not use such an idea. She had followed her feeling in this regard, for one does not know where the work is leading. It was leading back into nature, not forward into the man-made methods of life that oil wells would represent. On another level of work, an oil well may have been a good solution, but on this particular level of work it was necessary to wait and not jump at a solution. Such a jump actually leads nowhere. Here one sees the conscious choice, but one that is toned with feeling participation. The choice is not intellectually arbitrary, yet it is a choice. The selecting factor is then largely feeling evaluation, for the situation in which one is involved is an intense and emotional involvement that requires the whole being.

A man doing Active Imagination was faced with a colossus. Because he was so enormous, bestriding the world, further movement seemed impossible without the destruction of lesser things which were, by nature of the work, of great importance. He found himself in a frenzy. He was well aware that he was dealing with a situation having a directing influence on his life. It was not something to be dismissed lightly. Then it dawned on him with great relief that this was not a creature of human size, so it must be a god. With this, a new aspect of his problem had been revealed. Looking back, he wondered why he had not seen it earlier. But that is the point; one is in a situation and stews in it until enlightenment comes on yet another level. Only then is it real enlightenment with a specific message. Things become known on an entirely new level. It is this that makes Active Imagination so extraordinarily powerful.

Dr. Fordham points out in his book *The Objective Psyche* that Active Imagination helps in moving the analytical transference into a place where the patient is independent of the analyst. In this way it advances real maturity. This is also an important aspect of such work, for being a method used mainly in the advanced stages of analysis, it gives growing independence and a way usable in private life. Thus it terminates analysis in its stricter or more limited sense. It is a process demanding independent work and naturally a reduction of analytical hours, and thus leads to a greater dependence on the self. Then that which was so meaningful an analytical transference has a chance to develop into a real relationship and objective discussion of mutual interest. Thus the wisdom of the self replaces what in early analysis seemed to be the wisdom of the analyst.

In Yoga training, thoughts which flit have to be brought out of avidya (ignorance) and drawn together. This overcoming is the first step to growth. Western man is apt to think that the fantasies which flit into consciousness seem foolish, but if we consciously decide to let this fantasy flow and give it attention and value, that very attitude in itself has a marked effect, for, having our attention, they are no longer meaningless fleeting ideas or images, but the unconscious pours forth material which consciousness can begin to understand. This brings us at once to the question of how to deal with material produced, for in analysis the production in itself is insufficient to widen consciousness and increase understanding. A person's own interpretation is very important, but the material the unconscious has produced is always better understood by analogy.

By this I mean that mythology, legends, religious rituals, fairy tales, etc., offer material that can be used as amplification. This enhances the personal meaning, and, at the same time, the collective roots of such material are recognized. Baynes says that "the analogical method is indispensable in every psychological investigation. There could in fact be no extension of our scientific borders without it, only it must be tempered with a vigilant sense of reality, lest its reckless employment in an attempt to prove a thesis for which no real evidence is forthcoming bring the whole method into disrepute. In philosophy, history, and psychology, the analogical method has now been reinstated as a method par excellence, when properly employed, for gathering a new set of facts into a familiar container whose validity has been proved in an analogous field of study." [1]

I have found that if anyone has any doubt about the universal validity of what the unconscious has produced, amplification by analogy overcomes this, and through it one is better able to understand and accept the myth and mysteries of one's own soul. One can discover analogical material which forces one to accept

[1] H. G. Baynes, *Mythology of the Soul*, page 110.

one's connection with the whole human race and its intricate background.

The problem of psychological types also comes into any discussion on Active Imagination. It is natural that different people will have different approaches to the unconscious, while to some people any approach at all to psychic reality is difficult if not completely impossible. This largely depends on types, as Jung has shown in *Psychological Types*.

Some people take more naturally to Active Imagination than others and are able to develop symbolical thinking, that is, the image itself is granted a speaking-ness. However, quite apart from what is the superior function, whether it is thinking, feeling, sensation, or intuition, it takes on introverted attitude to allow the unconscious to speak. For the extravert, it is mainly the world which speaks. Jung says: "Active fantasies are called forth by intuition, that is, by an attitude directed toward the perception of unconscious contents in which the libido immediately invests all the elements emerging from the unconscious and, by means of association with parallel material, brings them to definition and plastic form."[2] He says further that "active fantasy owes its existence not merely to a one-sided intensive and antithetic unconscious process, but just as much to the propensity of the conscious attitude for taking up the indication or fragments of relatively lightly toned unconscious associations and developing them into complete plasticity by association with parallel elements. In the case of active fantasy then, it is not necessarily a question of a dissociated psychic state, but rather a positive participation of consciousness."[3] On the other hand a passive fantasy or dream can break through to consciousness without any conscious participation, thus bringing to light elements opposed to or not known by the conscious. These are the elements which can disrupt conscious attention by drawing off libido from the conscious ego. It is also part of the depressive condition which precedes real creativity.

One has to take the unconscious seriously, for this is more than aimless chatting with oneself, yet it is also true that sometimes the most meaningful work will commence in a spirit of

[2] C. G. Jung, *Psychological Types*, pages 574ff.
[3] Ibid.

fun, for in fun one co-operates in a well-meaning and non-critical way and gives free rein without prejudice. Then conscious co-operation adds meaning to the images and discerns the orientation of the unconscious. Experience shows us that the unconscious from one point of view is an energic process with "potential directedness." It contains the stuff on which consciousness itself is built and depends. Now some people have the most extraordinary difficulty in ascribing to the unconscious any serious goal or in fact any reality. A man once said, when asked to look at his dream seriously, that it must be the analyst's problem, since she, the analyst, could take a serious and guiding view of a dream. For him it was *only* a dream, a nothing but. Apart from the fact that anything being shrugged off as unimportant intimates its importance, one has to learn to accept responsibility toward the unconscious. Until one feels such responsibility the way is often clouded, and though the shifting of responsibility is human, it is, alas, sterile. The animal that appeared in this man's dream surely belonged in one sense to the archetypal non-personal realm, but this was *his* animal and the thing that required his understanding was his treatment of this symbolic image. The unconscious was throwing up an unpleasant truth which could lead nowhere when there was intellectual debunking. He was an extraverted sensation type to whom giving reality to the psyche was very difficult and for whom it would be a matter of long education. That education would not be an intellectual one. Experience is true knowledge. Jung has said that his "justification for speaking of the existence of unconscious processes at all is derived purely and solely from experience." [4]

It is clear now that Active Imagination is a conscious turning of attention to the unconscious, so it is a field where reductive interpretation of such images to the symptomatic does not apply, while a purposive interpretation sees such images as symbols which seek "with the help of existing material to a clear goal" and strive toward a future way of development. Jung says that "active fantasy being the principal attribute of the artistic mentality, the artist is not merely *representer*, he is also a *creator*, hence essentially an *educator* since his works have the value of symbols that trace out the line of future development. Whether

[4] Ibid., page 613.

the actual social validity of the symbol is more general or more restricted depends upon the quality or vital capacity of the creative individuality." [5] That is, the less fitted he is, the less the symbols will have universal validity, although that does not alter their value for him. In other words, when a highly symbolic work comes from the unconscious helped by conscious attention, the way will have been cleared of more or less personal elements, which allows of a symbolic rather than a symptomatic work to appear. Hence Active Imagination in its greatest capacity comes only in advanced stages of analysis and shows—and advances— maturity.

Plato has said that the world is a moving image of eternity, so that with imagination and intuition we remember something which has always been known, not something personal but something archetypal. We are drawn to these symbols because we also know. Somewhere we have known it because the arche- types speak out of the collective experience of soul. They are known yet "through a glass darkly." Jung points out that symbols used by art, real art, are not "private nor subjective but are a common language" which enables us to "communicate with the past and with the future as well as with contemporaries." [6] It is not the image but the psychic reality underlying the image which counts. The artist is somewhat different from others in that he uses all functions and often depends on his weakest for his expression. In Active Imagination one becomes the creative artist, although I do not mean by that that his work necessarily has professional value. It is often found that persons doing Active Imagination find an artistic mode of expression they had not used before. When it is the case of a person with a pronounced form of artistic expression, another is called into use, thus where the ego has to labor with a new form, it cannot steal the experience. The work which came under my notice and with which I will deal in the next chapters was done by an introverted intuitive who always had some form of artistic expression. It is the work done in the second half of life. When one's outer obligations to life have been fulfilled one can commence the spiritual quest.

She was quite conversant with metaphysical assumptions. Intellectually she had realized many great truths, but after doing a great deal of Active Imagination, this one small fantasy was produced which, when interpreted analogically, made a living experience of things which had been the experience of intuition. When one begins to know things in this way it is as if they grow up out of the body and one has knowledge on a different level. These are things we know, and it is the personal experience which makes them real. Jung says ". . . it must be mentioned that just as the human body shows a common anatomy over and above all racial differences, so, too, does the psyche possess a common sub-stratum. I have called the latter the collective unconscious. As a common human heritage, it transcends all differences of culture and consciousness and does not consist merely of contents capable of becoming conscious, but of latent dispositions toward identical reactions. Thus the fact of the collective unconscious is simply the psychic expression of identity of brain structure irrespective of all racial differences. By its means can be explained the analogy, going even as far as identity between various myth-themes and symbols, and the possibility of human understanding in general. The various lines of the psychic development start from one common stock whose roots reach back into the past. Here, too, lies the psychological parallelism with animals.

"Taken purely psychologically, it means that we have common instincts of ideation (imagination) and of action. All conscious imagination and action have grown out of these unconscious prototypes, and remain bound up with them." [7]

Much turns up in analysis that has reference directly to the personal life. When things cannot be seen from the personalistic angle, when a personalistic interpretation adds nothing and such interpretation can be harmful and even nonsensical, one is faced with things beyond the personal, in the realm of the non-personal psychic reality. Jung has said that "when something turns up in a dream (or Active Imagination) which has little or no connection with ordinary life, or something which does not exist in one's own life, you can be sure the unconscious has a tendency to convey something uncommon or extraordinary, its particular nature depending on the nature of the symbolism." [8]

[7] C. G. Jung and Richard Wilhelm, *Secret of the Golden Flower*, page 83.
[8] Ibid.

It is in this realm of the non-personal as such that the following work belongs, even though, in itself, it shapes the "individual" as all archetypal experiences do.

However, once something belonging to the collective unconscious is spoken, written, etc., it belongs to collective conciousness regardless of the individual. Thus it is necessary to work on the revelation of the unconscious so that the individual will not be trampled down or be merely used by it. By this I mean work done consciously will save him from falling into naïve unconscious thoughts or actions in which the ego is not taken into account. People can live archetypal lives. For instance, a man I knew lived the ideal of duty. Neither he nor his family could breathe naturally. He never saw the need to be humanly ordinary. The ego as an individual had been swallowed by an ideal. It was not until his wife and daughter left home that he came into the world long enough to recognize humanness. So relating such material to oneself, to one's conscious attitude, means getting into the picture humanly. That is why Active Imagination demands ego participation, so that one knows rather than remains merely an instrument of revelation. The writer of a fantasy must always ask himself his place in it. The final and important thing is not its collective value but what it means for him. Otherwise the value is lost in unconscious inflation. The material might reveal great collective values, but for the participant it is valuable in that it touches the experience of others and reveals again some age-old truths. No one can follow that revelation or make a system of it. An attempt to follow such a revelation and systematize it is, I think, the basis of many spurious sects. The revelation runs off with their reason, rather than being itself added to already valid conscious attitudes.

Therefore, it is apparent by now that Active Imagination cannot be copied. If a person has an experience, he is in the experience. If you try to follow another's experience, it is all outside and you are attempting to live another's experience and have no truth of your own.

In discussing Active Imagination one can only say this is an idea of how it is done; it is a tentative example. I can teach a person to paint, but his painting is not like mine, for his strokes, the very tension of his hands, produce a difference. And that difference is the important thing. *That* is his experience and his individual way, and I, even as teacher, cannot do it that way. So as analysts, we can only encourage and watch but never do it for another. There are no exact examples.

When an individual looks upon his work and applies it to himself he might say: "So this comes through me!" If he has a Christian heritage he might say: "I am a Christian with all this pre-Christian background. It is as if the whole of the growth of man is in me. I belong to the light and the darkness of nature, to the spiritual and material elements of human life. Yet all this was beyond my old conscious attitude." He knows it because it has happened *out* of him. Then he becomes more collective and at the same time more widened, more whole. He knows himself more fully and knows where things are greater than himself, that he has touched transcendent reality. His little conscious attitude is no longer the only thing. Then if he arrives at some sort of philosophy, it will be his own. It is not borrowed from another. In the long run, it is all subjective. Even though he is a grain of sand in the vast Sahara, he *is* that grain and his difference is that he has realized his connection with other grains and his importance to the whole, for the Sahara owes its existence to many such grains. However, within all is the secret mystery which cannot be conveyed without loss. No one reading a process of Active Imagination will grasp entirely what such a mystery meant to the person doing the work. And that is as it should be. Once a mystery is betrayed or vulgarized something of it is already lost. One can only indicate how things are, how things express themselves from the unconscious. No one can or should attempt anything more. As analysts, we can only bow our heads before a truth and a mystery which, as human beings, is beyond us also. While we cannot show the "how" of this work, we can help the person to enter and question the flow from the unconscious: we aid with conscious interference which brings the eternal drame intérieure to a conscious goal.

CHAPTER 3

The Beginning of the Myth: A Piece of Active Imagination with Commentary (The Old Man)

THIS MYTH commenced after a dream of a man the writer had known thirty years previously. The contemplation of the dream started the myth which she did not, at that stage, expect to go on further. But it was as if, once commenced, the unconscious forced itself through. The man she had dreamed about always seemed sad. She could recall no time when he had not given the impression of carrying an inexpressible sorrow. The question in her mind was why such a figure from so many years ago, and one with whom no contact had since been made, should appear. There was some meaning behind it which she turned to Active Imagination to discover. First a simple model was made in clay, and this was accompanied by a written fantasy which began as follows:

> There was once a man who was so sad he used to weep many tears. No one ever knew why he was sad and he was never able to tell anyone, for it seemed he could not express it. However since no one could ever understand, they all went off and left him with his sorrow.. He sat down and cried so much and for so long that his tears grew into a great lake which surrounded him.
> There he sat in the center of this great lake weeping and weeping. The trees grew up about the lake. The cattle came

by but they could not drink of the salt water, though they liked the tangy grass which sprang up along its banks.

The birds came down and lilted in and out of the water, and fish began to swim in its depths.

Then one day a little mermaid who had come out of the *saltiness* of the lake noticed the old man sitting in the center, crying. She went over and touched his eyes and he opened them.

"Why are you so sad?" she asked.

The man replied: "I have always had to suffer and to weep. There is no one with me. I am all alone."

"But," said the mermaid, "you are not alone. All of us live in your tears. If you had not suffered and cried, neither the fish nor I would have had a home."

"Then maybe I should not be sad," he said. "If you are all so happy, maybe I have something to be happy about." He commenced to rise up, and the mermaid said:

"No, please do not go. If you should stop crying there would be no lake, and we would not have a home. We would die in the sun."

"You mean I must not enjoy myself?"

"If you leave you are responsible, and then when you saw us all dead, that would make you unhappy all over again."

"You are right. It means I have to go on suffering. But it is better suffering, for it is so that you can live. If I left I would start weeping again and that would be more bitter suffering because of my guilt. Do not fear, I will suffer that you may live, but, living, please understand why I suffer."

With this resolution he closed his eyes and the tears poured forth and the mermaid felt sad. She swam back to the depths, and as she passed the fish she was deep in thought. This man had to suffer, and because she had come face to face with him and had been forced to beg him to continue, she would always be herself aware of suffering. And she knew that there would now be suffering within her own heart too.

Before making some psychological comments on this first passage of the fantasy, I feel it necessary to preface them with a few remarks.

Active Imagination, as either a therapeutic process or as a means of developing a wider consciousness, might seem to the reader not only unusual, but rather weird. Therefore I will clarify a point or two, so that the reader can go along with the material and not be hampered by his critical objections. Let me say first that there is a wall, a necessary wall between the conscious and the unconscious. This division is requisite in order that we may direct our lives to the best of our ability. The primitive has very little division between conscious and unconscious. Creative personalities give free rein to the unconscious. The more consciously directed life is, the less is known of the unconscious, which has its effect without this fact being recognized. The conscious attitude is always counterbalanced in the unconscious, so where the conscious is too one-sided, such unconscious processes that are a natural ebb and flow for the primitive and a lowered consciousness become intensified. Such intensified components can push into the conscious and have a disrupting effect. Or in some cases such irruptions are taken over by the conscious completely and without criticism and there is no counterbalance or constraint.

When a person uses a critical judgment toward himself he is dealing only with his conscious attitudes and not taking into account the regulating function of the unconscious. As you will see from the dream which commenced this Active Imagination, there was a certain depression of spirit suggested by the sad man. Therefore the dreamer, in order to let the whole theme develop, fell into the mood of the dream without reserve and noted down the fantasy this mood produced. This was done not as a "free association." The material did not leave the orbit of its beginning. Hence we arrive at a symbolic expression of the mood, a procedure that gives enrichments and clarification.

All critical attention has been eliminated, so elements that in some way had been gathered together in the mood that started the procedure were revealed. Since these underlying motifs have been given free rein and conscious uncritical attention, they begin to articulate some fundamental concepts of mankind. There was obviously a motive for such an undertaking, and the unconscious had the will to take the lead. This condition is not always present and, indeed, seems never to be present in some people.

Only later will the ego take the real lead in coming to terms with the unconscious material. This is necessary, for the unconscious is not to be taken literally but rather its meaning clarified to the satisfaction of the individual. I will not be concerned here with what comes from this *Auseinandersetzung*, for this is always unique and personal. All I do is present a piece of work as evidence of the process on a deep level. What is valid for one person is not necessarily so for another. Therefore I hope the reader can follow the material with objective interest and not take it personalistically or become besieged by philosophical or intellectual prejudices. I merely present the material and analogy; fall victim to expressing something of its psychological message in places; and claim the content of the fantasy as neither true nor false but merely as another example of how things are in the unconscious. Its individual import has to do only with the writer of the fantasy.

This is the first portion of a simple fantasy in which a mermaid is created and responds to her creator. Beneath it, we see the age-old story of creation which has been told and retold in many ways. It is more than a creation myth, for as we continue we will see that it expresses in its own way the origin and growth of consciousness with the many sacrifices that such growth demands.

In the figure of the old man one sees a sort of unconscious chaos; there is emotion and longing, and out of this longing something is born. Psychologically, it is the sadness and depression that precede creativity, a condition forever existent when libido is drawn into the unconscious. Every creative artist knows the sadness, emotion, and longing which precedes his creation. It is an archetypal situation inherent in the creative urge where man unites with his creator. The old man is the god longing for his creation, a creation in which to fulfill himself. The circle of tears in which he sat is on one hand an unconscious state and on the other the all-embracing nature of the deity from which something could emerge. The man is the unconscious totality [1] and the water in which he sits is his all-embracing nature. His sadness is an unspecific yearning. Not until the woman or mermaid emerged could he achieve a conscious state. The creator must have a realizer in order to exist for someone. Prior to her emergence,

[1] C. G. Jung, *Aion*, page 212.

there was one unconscious totality, then she with her question started things moving for both of them. She is the question in the heart of the god who needs man in order to be known, as if God becomes conscious through ego consciousness. The woman as mermaid is a dawning consciousness, a core of being, the developing form or concept of God's consciousness.

The sea was called by Pythagoras the tear of Saturn. Within its dark depths are unknown forces. In the fantasy, birds lilted in and out of these waters. It is spiritual intuition penetrating the darkness of the unconscious, and the birds would also be a symbol of Sophia, who was with God "from the beginning." [2] Birds always have a spiritual connotation. The fantasy continues to say that fish began to swim in the depths of the lake, so there was movement and life in this great unconscious force. The fish itself has widespread symbolic meaning with which Dr. Jung has dwelt extensively in *Aion*.

There is a distinct connection between the old man in the fantasy and the Babylonian culture god Oannes, who was a fish. Khidir, the Persian god of green and growing things, was born from the water where the fish disappeared when a search was being made for the fountain of eternal life. He, like Oannes, was a veiled god, the veil proclaiming their divine wisdom. The photograph of the model of the old man which was made while the fantasy was being written shows this figure is veiled. The unconscious brings up again those ideas which have been known before, and in many ways, for the old man is also a veiled god. He is the "old man of the sea," who, when grasped, can lead to the discovery of the soul (Helen).[3] He comes again and again, changing from form to form, from vapor to fire. He has to be seized quickly in order that he will reveal his secret wisdom. The whereabouts of "Helen" was the secret of the old man of the sea, Proteus, and, as we will see after confrontation by the mermaid (the yet half-conscious one), he, the old man of our fantasy, revealed the whereabouts of Wisdom, the old woman who ordained the world.

The old man is the center of the lake. He is both the center and the beginning; surrounded by waters which have flowed out

[2] *Proverbs* 8:22ff. Sophia is the Wisdom of God.
[3] Homer's *Odyssey*.

of him, he is an archetypal symbol of God. When we speak of a symbol or an image of God it in no way is a metaphysical statement of what God is. It is an image that conveys the idea of the center and the beginning. To him belongs the ocean, the unconscious in which there is already the salt from which the mermaid comes into being. We have a picture of the longing which was within the god beginning to stir and take form. This is the feminine creating side contained in the godhead and from whom it was necessary to separate in order to be known. To remain within this unconscious totality is uncreative, while to separate is the beginning of progress. Only after separation can relatedness begin. In actual life, it is true that a woman caught by the animus, who lives in the realm of the masculine gods (which is often the fate of modern women where the greatest stress is laid on Logos and the masculine principle) cannot really relate, for Eros values are given no credit. She has to be separated from the Logos gods and born again into the Eros realm.

The mermaid is the life which came from the sea. This sea had carried within itself the latent human. In this way the history of evolution before man existed is touched. In other words, when life first stirred in the waters, man was potentially there. Here, of course, we enter the realm of intuition and of potential life connected with "the Word."

It is, however, not only said the woman came from the lake, but specifically that she came from the *saltiness* of the lake. This suggests qualitativeness, that she embodies a quality of the old man, which would be quite in keeping with general religious ideas. In his book *Psychology and Alchemy*, Jung quotes from the Rosarium, an alchemical text of the middle fifteenth century, the following: "'Who therefore knows the salt and its solution, knows the hidden secret of the wise men of old. Therefore turn your mind upon the salt for in it alone [that is the mind] is the science concealed and is the most excellent and the most hidden secret of all ancient philosophers.'" Jung enlarges this by saying: "The Latin text has 'in ipsa sola' referring therefore to 'mens' [mens = mind]. One would have to assume a double misprint were the secret after all concealed in the salt. But as a matter of fact 'mind' and 'salt' are close 'cousins—cum grano salis! Hence, according to Khunrath (who was a medieval alchemist), salt is not only the physical center of the earth, but at the same time the sal sapientiae of which he says: 'Therefore direct your feeling, senses, reason and thought upon the salt alone.' The anonymous author of the Rosarium says in another place that the work must be performed 'with true and not fantastic imagination,' and that the stone will be found when the 'search lies heavily on the searcher.' " [4]

In Miss Hannah's lecture on Polarities of the Psyche [5] she spoke of the fact that Jung had, in his book *Mysterium Coniunctionis*, brought together a number of quotations to show that salt is represented in alchemy as bitter, solving, as origin of colors and that it was regarded as feminine, and from all this he drew the conclusion that salt is a symbol of differentiated feeling, relatedness (Eros) supported by Wisdom. He says: "A confirmation of our interpretation of salt as Eros—that is, feeling relatedness—is also given by the fact that the bitterness is the origin of the colors. As can be seen from the drawings and paintings of patients to accompany their analysis by Active Imagination, colors represent feeling values. One often observes that at first only a pencil or pen is used with the purpose of preserving fleeting sketches of dreams, intuitions, and fantasies. But from a certain moment on, the patient begins to use color and indeed from that very moment when a merely intellectual interest is replaced by a feelingful participation. Occasionally one sees the same phenomena in dreams which become definitely colorful in such a moment. . . ." [6]

As a feminine or Eros creature, then, the mermaid was the feeling relatedness expressed by salt, and, as Jung has pointed out in *Mysterium Coniunctionis*, supported by Wisdom. This is borne out later by the fantasy itself, showing how the unconscious connects quite naturally those things which have always been connected.

All those who are acquainted with salt beds know how they

[4] C. G. Jung, *Psychology and Alchemy*, page 244 (bracketed insertions are mine).

[5] Miss Hannah, C. G. Jung Institute, 1955.

[6] C. G. Jung, *Mysterium Coniunctionis*, page 248.

sparkle and reflect vividly all changing hues from dawn to dusk. Emerging from this saltiness, she is not only essence and center, but this feminine being reflects the colorful nature of the god. The changes in the color of a salt bed are affected by the sun's rays. The sun is consciousness or Logos, which gives life to Eros. These two principles of life, sun (Logos) and moon (Eros) are interdependent. This immediately leads us to another motif of the fantasy. The mermaid touched the eyes of the old man.

The eyes in mythology are often representatives of sun and moon. "The eyes of the Lord which run to and fro through the whole earth." [7] In Buddhist Nisattwa Manjveri the sun and moon are God's eyes. In Egypt the sun was regarded as the creator of man. The sun's eyes were torn out and fell to earth to create man. In some ancient myths Adam's eyes were made from the sun and the moon when God gathered the four corners of the earth together to create him. The opening of the eyes in the fantasy was an important act. Like ancient myths, this does not speak of the creating of physical being, but rather speaks of the origin of consciousness. It is here one touches the childhood of mankind. In this connection Jung says: "Logos and Eros are intellectually formulated intuitive equivalents of the archetypal images of Sol and Luna. In my view the two luminaries are so descriptive and so superlatively graphic in their implications that I would prefer them to the more pedestrian terms Logos and Eros, although the latter do pin down certain psychological peculiarities more aptly than the rather indefinite 'Sol and Luna.' The use of these images requires at any rate an alert and lively fantasy, and this is not an attribute of those who are inclined by temperament to purely intellectual concepts. These offer us something finished and complete, whereas an archetypal image has nothing but its naked fullness, which seems inapprehensible by the intellect. Concepts are coined and negotiable values; images are life." [8]

It was from touching eyes which opened and permitted the realization of her existence that she knew there was something other than herself. By awareness of this otherness she became

[7] Zechariah 4:10.

[8] Jung, op. cit., page 180.

separated from God. That is the first fall. The sun and the moon from whose tears she was begotten were also her awakening.[9] In much the same way as man is the small, seemingly personal carrier of the Logos principle, which is a principle transcending him in its universal validity, so also is he illuminated by the Eros principle, which is also transcendent and belongs to the realm of God. In the myth, the mermaid's first reaction was feeling, and later in the myth a heart was bestowed upon her by the goddess Wisdom. Logos and Eros are principles belonging in the realm of the great mystery man lives. They come to him as it were from outside and are, the fantasy suggests, bestowed by the gods. These attributes are the gift within creation and thus appear inherent in man.

Emerging from the lake and becoming active on her own behalf, the mermaid became a feeling being and recognized sadness. In the process of growth of consciousness man has been torn from the arms of nature and unconsciousness. It is a process felt as sadness and as guilt. In the course of this emergence, man is forced to distinguish "I" from the "other." Being forced out of what Levy Bruhl has designated "participation mystique" he feels the guilt and sadness of separation.[10] To become independent is also a responsibility and is in opposition to his original condition. He has to become a god-man, a Logos creature, when he is apart and responsible. So the fantasy says the mermaid was happy in unconsciousness until she encountered another and became herself conscious.

[9] Sol and Luna are male and female and represent also conscious and unconscious. In alchemy the sun was gold and the moon was silver.

[10] Every act of culture is a break with nature and one can only safely return to nature on a higher level of being, thus acknowledging the oneness rather than be unconsciously contained in it. As Jung has pointed out, if unconsciousness were the best condition the primitive would be in an ideal state, whereas he is filled with strange fears and superstitions. What one can render back to the Deity is the oneness on a higher level. There is also the truth that to remain in an unconscious state because of parental fixation also brings guilt because of the denial of life. Man has raised himself against nature (as a child must raise itself against the parents) because it was a demand within nature itself, to a state both god-defying and god-like. This very situation has led man to a godless condition where credit is given to the intellect and to reason and where the irrational feminine and the oneness of nature are denied.

When the old man realized others were happy he suggested happiness for himself, but this would have meant the death of the mermaid. If he took over the role of his creatures there would be no separation, and consciousness would be lost again. There must be a separation between god and man. She had achieved some realization, so she had to beg him to give her the right to live while he remained in his misery. Out of an unbearable condition we create something better. Contentment never forces man to exert himself. Now he had a reality with a new meaning in which he desired to participate. She could neither go back nor give in, and it is true in life, one cannot turn back. She had asked a question of her creator and been caught in it as we are caught by the consciousness we have gained.

Jung has said that whoever knows God has an effect upon him and that "existence is only real when it is conscious to somebody. That is why the creator needs conscious man . . . for utter loneliness and longing would accompany the torture of nonexistence."[11] The mermaid was the product of the god's feminine side, the saltiness inherent in him, and by her willingness to suffer the guilt, she caught them both into the drama of life. The feminine principle or the created world has always borne the responsibility for suffering. The mermaid was the special creation set apart by the god for his destiny. In life, it is the task in individuation of the individual, to learn he is a special creation and responsible for the destiny of God. Jung says: "If one takes the doctrine of predestination literally, it is difficult to see how it can be fitted into the framework of the Christian message. But taken psychologically, as a means to achieving a definite effect, it can readily be understood that these references to predestination give one a feeling of distinction. If one knows one has been singled out by divine choice and intention from the beginning of the world, then one feels lifted beyond transitoriness and meaninglessness of ordinary human existence and transported to a new state of dignity and importance like one who has a part in the divine world drama. In this way man is brought nearer to God, and this is in entire accord with the meaning of the message in the Gospels."[12]

[11] C. G. Jung, *Answer to Job*, pages 16ff.
[12] Ibid., page 73.

CHAPTER **4**

The Myth with Commentary continued
(The Old Woman)

THE MERMAID swam to the man and said: "Life is no longer what it used to be. No longer can I be content to gather the sea flowers for my garden. I suffer always a pain in my heart, and I desire to know what is beyond the sea. I wonder where you came from and I am no longer content."

The man opened his eyes and looked at her compassionately. "I too am condemned," he said, "yet I have accepted to remain as I am that you might live."

"Yes, I know. That is part of my suffering also, but not all of my sorrow. I was born from your tears as Eve was born from the rib of Adam, but it has not made me happy to know it. In my original state I was happy."

"You came with curiosity and touched my eyes and we both are more unhappy. Yet mine is a sadness with a purpose."

"You say it is all my doing . . . well, there is a purpose in my sadness too. I long, and once I did not know what longing was. Yet for what I long I do not know, for it is all so far away. I am confined and I do not want to be confined."

The old man looked thoughtful, then said: "Go and swim three times around the lake and then tell me what you see."

The mermaid obeyed, and when she had nearly finished the third round nothing had happened. She threw herself upon the

44

rock near to the edge of the lake and cried aloud. "I am and I am not . . . and it is the fault of the man." She cried so bitterly that it sounded like the sighing of the wind in the trees. Then came a voice.

"Why are you so sad, mermaid?"

For a moment she was afraid to look up. Once she had said just that to the man. So after a struggle with fear she looked up through her tears. An old woman sat upon the rocks, knitting. "I do not know," ventured the mermaid, "except that I long; except that my heart breaks with its hurting; and I can no longer be what I was."

"Then what is it you would want to be?" asked the old woman.

The mermaid thought awhile. "Anything. I will accept whatever happens."

"Maybe what will happen is that you will remain just what you are."

"No," she cried, "no, I cannot take that. You see"—she looked at the woman consideringly—"I am not as you or the man. I am neither a woman nor a fish.

"You have a woman's suffering heart."

"Can that help me?"

"Yes, if you accept the fire which burns in it."

The mermaid looked puzzled. "Who are you?" she asked.

"I am she who knitted the world, stitch by stitch. Like the man, I am committed. With these two needles I do the work, yet if I stopped, things would come to an end."

"Then you must know many things."

"Yes," said the woman, "I am 'Wisdom.' One day I knitted a heart, and because it was you who asked a question it became your heart."

"And it became a man's suffering, too. . . ."

Wisdom nodded her head.

"What," said the mermaid, edging nearer, "do you think I should do?"

"Not even I can advise you," said Wisdom. "The problem is yours. When you commence asking questions it never seems to end. Your heart will tell you best what you want."

"I want to go onto the land among the trees, and not die from the scorching sun. But above all I would like wings so that I could soar to the sky and get to know everything."

"You ask a great deal," said Wisdom.

"My heart requires a lot, for it hurts so much."

"Then take this cord," said Wisdom. "Go back to the man and sleep near the rocks at his feet, but first tie the cord about you."

The mermaid took the cord and folded it about her. "Will you be here when I return?" she asked.

"I will be here."

The next morning when the mermaid awoke she felt something strange. She looked up at the man, and as she moved toward him she discovered she had the wings of a bird. So great was her delight, she forgot the man and stretched the wing in the morning breeze. She rose up in the air and flashed over mountain and stream, over city spires and country valleys. On and on she went, ever joyous, ever rising higher and sometimes circling lower.

At last she felt weary, and when she saw birds sitting in the trees, she decided to join them. She folded her wings to alight, but she had to cling to the branches with her hands. She tried to put her fish body on the bough, but it would not stay. Her wings were tired, and now her arms ached also. Wearily she dropped to the ground. She felt hot and uncomfortable.

"Oh, how can I get home," she cried, and a snake passing by paused to look at her. . . . "If you cling to my back," he said, "I will take you along part of the way with me."

"It's having these wings," she explained. "I think I went too far."

"Most people with wings do," replied the snake. "Why didn't you ask for legs?"

"I wanted something better."

"If you wanted something better, you should have asked for her wisdom and her immortal soul. Then you could be human if you wanted to be. But that is not easy. They are full of fiery and begetting passions, and always seeking their immortality in God, and building spires and churches. You know, if I were you, I would go back to the deep water. Human life is all so much struggle. You can make yourself happy in your shell garden."

"No, I cannot. Besides, there is the man."

"Well, he did it himself."

"No, not exactly. I am never quite sure about that."

"That is the sort of doubt that humans have. Here is where I must leave you."

"But how will I get along?"

"You will manage."

She tried her wings again but they were too weary to lift her. The sun was scorching her so she crept to some shade, wondering how far it was to her lake. Then a bird flew down.

"If you care to hold my legs," he said, "I could give you a lift over the range to your lake."

Delighted, the mermaid clung to him. . . . "You know," he said, "I would not believe the snake entirely. I do not think you are doing things the right way, but I believe you have the right desires in your heart. Why don't you have another talk with Wisdom?" he suggested, lowering her to the little island where the man sat weeping.

"All I want," she said, "is to go to sleep. The heat of the earth, the weariness of flying are too much for me."

She slipped down the rocks to the cool water, thinking how comfortable it would be in her bed of seaweed, but try as she would she could not go down, for her wings would bear her up out of the water. She struggled and struggled, then in despair she drifted to the edge of the lake and cried again.

"Why," asked Wisdom, "do you cry again? . . . Have you not the wings you want and have you not learned many things?"

The mermaid hung her head. "Oh, indeed I have. I love the sky and the trees, yet I belong nowhere. I am neither bird nor beast nor fish. I cannot rest with birds of the air nor walk upon the land, and now no longer can I remain in the depths of the sea. There is no rest for me. If you would not mind, I wish you would take these wings back."

"They will drop off now you have realized they are of no use to you."

"And yet, Wisdom, I do not want just to swim in the sea. I have seen so much."

"What is it you want most?"

"All your wisdom and all your power so that I can do just as I want."

"That," said Wisdom, "no one can have."

"Will you tell me who gave all this power and all this wisdom to you?"

"I just am. But you see nothing is for one person alone. Even I share that which I have."

"Am I asking too much? The serpent suggested I should, and that I should ask not only for those, but also for immortality."

Wisdom smiled. "Everyone asks too much at times. But it is good not to want everything for oneself."

The mermaid swam around, thinking. What could she desire that would not be for herself alone? Then when she had conceived an idea she went straight to Wisdom.

"If you would give me two legs," she said, "I could live on the land and then the man would be free. He would not have to sit all day and cry so that I may live. I am sure that it would be better that way."

"May be," said Wisdom, "but is this really for the man?"

The mermaid hung her head again. "Well, it is mostly for me."

Wisdom smiled compassionately. "Then I will tell you what to do. Go to the swordfish and ask him to open your breast, then you must take out your heart and offer it to the man."

"Oh, I cannot. I would die. I cannot and I will not sacrifice my heart to the man."

"You came from his tears and he continues to weep for you. You know what it is like to suffer, and this sacrifice will save him."

"But it is not the solution I wanted. I did want something for myself as well."

She swam away then, going around and around the lake and as she swam she thought, "I will go on doing this always and the man will go on crying always, for he has promised to do that. Nothing, nothing can ever come out of it."

So with a great effort she approached the swordfish who, with his great sharp spear, rent open her bosom. Then she swam to the man, and as her blood colored the water, she rent out her heart and offered it up to him. . . .

"Here is my heart. The life you gave me I offer back to you. You can live without suffering. It seems foolish that we should both go on in this everlasting circle. I must have a place and a

purpose, and it seems this is my purpose. Please do not cry for
me, for my sacrifice would then have been in vain."

The old man took the heart she offered up to him, and the mermaid sank into the waters at his feet.

There was a great storm on the lake; the lightning flashed and
the winds blew and the rain came down until the lake was so full
it made a river that stretched to the sea.

Then the old man stood erect and took the mermaid in his
arms. Her heart had grown so large it became a castle upon the
rocks, and within this castle he laid the mermaid down.

Soon she opened her eyes and looked about. Seeing the man,
she said, "I am dead. I have given my heart away. I did not know
I would ever know anything more. Tell me, is this the heaven of
the immortals?"

"May be," said the old man, "may be."

Then she looked down at herself and saw she was a woman and
she rose up and moved about."This then is death," she whispered.

"This then is life," he replied.

"But how can it be? What of my heart?"

"That," said the man, "encompasses both of us. Wisdom has
given you a new heart. Nothing you sacrifice is really lost. It is
only changed. But had you known that, it would not have been
the same and there could have been no sacrifice."

"Wisdom said she would give me a little of her wisdom . . .
but not all of it."

"Ah, yes, but first a new heart that you may be able to contain
and endure it."

"Yes, I must endure the becoming," she said.

After the writer of the fantasy had completed this portion,
she had a dream that a silver horse sprang from her heart. She
was awakened with a pounding that lasted some days, a fact that
shows the effect of such a close contact with the psyche. Although
this whole work is projected much as alchemical writings, and
does not refer to personal psychology as such, the loving participation really has effect. The mermaid-woman always seems to act as
an ego. She is in one way the ego of the unconscious, the heroine
who takes the journey and unites other aspects of the psyche with
her. She is the vessel through whom Wisdom and later Wisdom's

shadow function and show their unity. She does not coincide with ego, but is an archetype of the self who was coexistent with God.[1]

A little consciousness had made the agony of remaining in unconsciousness unbearable, so the mermaid consults the man about it.[2] When she makes her claim as to the intolerable condition, he immediately lays the blame upon her. In analysis, this is recognized as a trick of the animus, who pushes one on one hand and blames one about it on the other. So much has suffering strengthened her, she is able to stand up to him, for one pushes ahead out of a need which does not exist when things are comfortable. He did not know what to do, for he himself was depending upon her for consciousness in the more human realm. Nature composed of opposites within itself must always depend on man to bring in the human equation. Solomon points to the need of the human equation when he shows that Wisdom's sister (Prov. 7:21) entices man in the way of worldly wisdom while Wisdom herself (Prov. 8:22) exalts spiritual wisdom. Between the two the human prerogative seems to be choice. We will see in the story that the mermaid will gradually be forced from unconsciousness to exercise the human prerogative of choice and its consequent responsibility. So the old man suggests she swim three times around the lake, for the soul must find the way which is not obvious nor can be determined by logos. Three is a dynamic number and it is a common motif in fairy tales to have to try three times. It is a struggle between the masculine and feminine and is also a test of endurance, for surely it is useless to attain what one has not the capacity to endure. It is not unexpected that after traversing

[1] The fact of her desire for consciousness and also that she sprang from the tears of the man, Deity, show that the quest she undertakes is that of the deity himself. Man's growth of consciousness and knowledge is not, as is often assumed, entirely his own act. It is also that which is acting through him, of which he is the instrument and servant. No matter how divine and free he assumes himself to be, he is in the service of another.

[2] The heroine is the abstract feminine. She is the self which patterns ego. She is not an individual but an archetype common to humanity. This general disposition points to a self figure. The self is that which is inherent and the ego is the instrument of the self. She behaves as an ego. She is the common substratum of all egos. The ego also has that which is common to all egos.

three times around the lake she arrives at the fourth. She discovers the feminine Sophia or Wisdom who is sitting upon the rocks and so has contact with the feminine creating principle, the one who has been operative without her knowledge.

Wisdom in Proverbs 8 says of herself:

The Lord possessed me in the beginning of his way, before his works of old.
I was set up from everlasting, from the beginning, or ever the earth was.
When there were no depths, I was brought forth; when there were no fountains abounding with water.

When he established the heavens, I was there,

When he marked out the foundations of the earth, then I was by him, as a master workman, and I was daily his delight, rejoicing always before him,
Rejoicing in his habitable earth;
And my delight was with the sons of men.[3]

In Ecclesiasticus she describes herself as Logos or the word of God. "I came out of the mouth of the most high."[4] Wisdom or Sophia is the breath or pneuma of feminine nature which existed before the "Dawn." She, as spirit, moved upon the waters of the beginning. Her joy is in the sons of men and as "psychopomp" she leads the way to God. Jung says of her: "She is indeed the 'master workman'; she realizes God's thoughts by clothing them in material form, which is the prerogative of all feminine beings. Her coexistence with Yahweh signifies the perpetual hieros gamos from which the worlds are begotten and born."[5]

It is important, even essential in a woman's psychology that Wisdom should be active in realizing and materializing, in this case knitting together the thoughts of God. Wisdom is weaving the world from the nature of God. This is an archetypal situation underlying the feminine principle, for in life it seems a woman's

[3] *Proverbs* 8:22-24.
[4] *Ecclesiasticus* 24.
[5] C. G. Jung, *Answer to Job*, page 55.

lot to be busy bringing something about. She often sees more than a man, since she stands in the place where he is most blind, unless he is aware of the intricate weaving inherent in his own feminine side. Jung says in *Answer to Job*: "If we consider Jahwe's behavior up to the reappearance of Sophia, one indubitable fact strikes us—the fact that his actions are accompanied by an inferior consciousness. Time and time again we miss reflection and regard for absolute knowledge." [6] . . . "A situation rises in which reflection is needed. That is why Sophia steps in. She reinforces the much needed self-reflection and thus makes possible Jahwe's decision to become man." [7]

The woman confronts the man with the fact that she could no longer remain confined, and it is Wisdom who has given her the heart whereby she enters into the masculine-feminine struggle. Things must now really be experienced, for it is the materializing side of God that has forced the issue, and so she begins to remind the god of his responsibility toward her. In asking for the change, the mermaid tells Wisdom that her heart requires a lot because it hurts so much. This heart which gave the pain was the gift of Wisdom herself. Who was responsible, the creator or the created? The old woman, Wisdom, is an archetype with no real compassion for the frailty of the human heart. It has been bestowed, so from then on it is the responsibility of the recipient. At the same time Wisdom tells her that her heart will tell her what to do. She had given her something of value. As something of us is in what we do, she, Wisdom, was herself within the gift she had made. She was not a power outside or far away, but actually within the heart she had created. So what the woman does as an embodiment of the essence (salt) of the old man, she does also for Wisdom. Thus Wisdom can place the responsibility for a wish which was ultimately granted squarely upon her. She received the wings, the spirit which lifted her beyond the confines of the lake. She was

[6] Ibid., page 67.

[7] Ibid., page 69.

N.B. Jewish Gnosis: God suffered from a headache because of loneliness. There was tension, lightning, and the first sun was created.

Hindu: God was lonely, suffering, and bored, and created the world like a toy.

Tantric: God is always accompanied by Shakti and could not create without her. She realizes and creates the world from the dreams of Shiva.

granted a gift for which she was not prepared. In spite of the wings she still had a fish tail! The fish tail is the unconscious aspect that drags as a weight on consciousness. Its non-human aspect must be redeemed for it to function helpfully. Psychologically, it means that too much intuition can be wings which carry us above reality, and thus on the side of reality (and the sensation function) we can remain far too unconscious, a fact which makes life too unbalanced. Again, to fly close to the sun (Logos) means for the feminine to be burned by the rays of the masculine principle and to be unable to find shelter in the moonlight of Eros. To have wings (consciousness) and a fish tail (unconsciousness) is too much tension.

˅ At this point the serpent emerged. He represents the earthy or chthonic life. He is the one who has learned to live on earth. As with his encounter with Eve, he had no real intention of dissuading her from consciousness or progress, but on the contrary planted in her the seeds of further demands. He widened her horizons, inspired her, and fanned the fire of desire for the things she had glimpsed. The serpent knew, as when he tempted Eve, that the feminine creating principle requires only a glimpse at something "beyond" to move it into action. So having made such big statements, his advice to sit quietly in her shell garden was as effective as asking a cat to sit in an aviary and eat grapes. There was no stopping the flow of things begun, no possibility now to stop the creative will from expression.

Why, we might ask, is it the serpent who, earthy himself, fills her with aspirations? The serpent represents a Mercurius, a chthonic god, who lifted her out of an unbearable condition because the sun was scorching her. The sun, as we know, is, psychologically, a Logos symbol. Thinking and intuition were touched by the fire of heaven. She had seen the world from on high, had been in the depths, but was not yet feelingly and actually involved. In life, the intuitive, if he does not watch, can grasp so much that things have to be brought back to earth or he has missed the vital experience. Any superior function has to be sacrificed if a wider, deeper experience of life is demanded. Safely on the earth one is in a better position to seek shelter from the sun. Too much intuition and too much conscious knowledge can burn one up, for these are not the transforming fires that come from the deep places where the genii tend the furnace and bring about the transformation of animal nature into something that can be lived humanly. The serpent as earth and light bringer suggested things which would lead her into danger and into life, and then left her. That is the typical serpent act. He crosses her path and she is expelled from heaven, for he symbolizes also the "fall from grace." But as he did with Eve, he performs his function in order to get things moving out of a static infertile condition, a paradise of unconsciousness. He is the instigator toward consciousness, toward experience rather than intuition.

Then what follows? The bird flew down. He is the "Holy Ghost," the individual love, the dove of Sophia and Aphrodite who saw things from a different place from that of the serpent. Being the bird of Aphrodite, the spirit consonant with feminine deities, he knew the best course was to seek knowledge from Wisdom, who was herself the Eros of God, the feminine principle. Only she who had to do with the cause of the distress was in a position to offer help. The idea is, psychologically, that he whom the father (or mother) has ruined, only the father (or mother) can restore.

The mermaid could not rid herself of her wings. When one has emerged so far out of unconsciousness it is difficult and sometimes impossible to go back. The more consciousness one has achieved, the more one is separated from the instincts that give indications of the secret wisdom of God. To know God means to know also the instincts, to find the two ends of the spectrum. She is caught in her own growth and is faced with an alternative—to sacrifice or remain in an unbearable condition. The sacrifice is expiatory. It is a demand from the dark side of Nature for extension both up and down, that the heavenly God might incarnate. It is the great extremity which precedes every step forward; an extremity from which man can break or enter a new psychological dimension and take up consciously the burden of being "marked by God."

Her next request was for two legs, and as she saw it, if she could get these she would relieve the old man of his responsibility and also release herself from her own responsibility to her creator. This is the great inclination of the modern age. Yet if she went off on her own it could scarcely solve the problem of his loneliness. His expectations were indissolubly bound up with her, that one whose very developing individual nature made it possible for her to be willing to leave him. That is so often forgotten or not realized, life is unique for every individual yet never independent, for one is responsible to life itself. When Wisdom asked her to sacrifice her life she brought her at once into a condition of reflection. Reflection is the human quality par excellence. It is that which lifts man above the animals and purely animal reactions. Through this demand of Wisdom, she was able to contemplate the whole situation, to evaluate and decide. As a result of this reflection a change was brought about. Reflection lifted her from a half-animal to a human realm. Reflection paved the way for her transformation, a transformation brought about by the sacrifice of the gift she had received from Wisdom. It was a gift made especially for her and bestowed, which is important, on her at a moment of ego consciousness, that is, at the time she had asked a question.

Wisdom and the old man are archetypal figures and thus can demand sacrifices, for in the hierarchy of gods they are bound by no human values or human pity. They leave it to the *human* to redeem nature to humanness. In succumbing to their suggestion, the mermaid shows a newfound insight. There are things in nature about which one can do nothing, for one is up against forces and seemingly powerless. She sees the uselessness of a situation out of which nothing grows. Hers was a special birth which must be sacrificed. It was not ecstatic love, but the result of consideration which is already a widened consciousness. Of Sophia it can be said that "sacrifice and suffering are prerequisites of the transformation conferred by her, and this law of dying and becoming is an essential part of wisdom of the Great Goddess of living things, the Goddess of all growth, psychic as well as physical." [8]

The sacrifice of the heart is the first of the sacrifices incurred in the fantasy and seems, as it were, a total sacrifice. It was the surrendering of her most precious possession, her life, with no possibility of getting anything in return. It was a propitiation to neither the old man nor Wisdom, and had no secret taint of receiving. It was the sacrifice of her total possession. To give up the heart is also to give up ego ownership. We say "I have an inspiration." That is, an idea has come to us. It came without

[8] Erich Neumann, *The Great Mother*, page 252.

effort and it is a hubris to claim it as a possession of the ego. In exactly the same way one has a feeling which takes one over and belongs in the realm of Eros as much as intuition belongs in the realm of Logos. It is just here even more than with an intuition that the ego lays claim to it. To claim this feeling for the ego is equally a hubris which has ultimately to be sacrificed to the principle of Eros. Eros, feeling-relatedness, had been bestowed by Wisdom from the essence of the god. She came from salt, which was designated as feeling-relatedness. The ego can only lay claim to the possession of feeling until such egotistical ideas are surrendered to the gods.

It is also a psychological truth that the ego must die before the self can become an actual experience. St. Thomas Aquinas said that "no creature attains to a further grade of nature without ceasing to exist." It is a problem that one encounters in analysis that old values have to be given up if one is to continue further. Often it is a heroic sacrifice which, unsuspected, is destined to lift one on to a different level, away from an old repeating cycle. The serpent as demon in the fantasy is the one who says go back to the shell garden and, as such, is the power demon who attaches great importance to unconsciousness and inactivity. It is the power of darkness opposed to light. Inactivity is often idealized as a feminine role, as passivity that awaits fulfillment, whereas it is the Eros activity of woman that brings transformation to both herself and the male. Sophia Wisdom may not curl up in sleep or there would be no creating and awakening principle. The mermaid chose the darkness of death, something which seemed final and where her intuitions gave her no guiding light. She evaluated the situation, and reality (sensation) saw it as inevitable. The threshold of growth is annihilation.

The attempt is made in blind humility. She suffered and sacrificed, but blindly and honestly. That is the great test in analysis, to trust oneself blindly to the unknown when all seems hopeless. Laziness and a sense of impossibility can swamp one; they are the demons which lead to unconsciousness. But it is just here if one tries that things begin to move, for the attitude in itself brings a flux of energy in its wake: the energy that is the new life and the transformation.

Up until now, Wisdom is very active and assigns the woman

her tasks much as Aphrodite demanded great undertakings from Psyche.[9] For woman it is necessary that her tasks and sacrifices are designed by the Great Mother or she may be in danger of surrendering in the wrong place. The tasks of Eros are those which make her strong in her own principle. Only then can she unite properly with Logos. When a woman surrenders to Logos without strength in her own principle, she is lost in what modern psychology refers to as being in the grip of the animus.

It seems necessary before passing on to note the connection between the serpent, the swordfish, and the dove. They are all Mercurius figures.[10] The serpent is a Lucifer who forces one to enlightenment through punishment, and the swordfish with his single horn is also a Mercurius. The dove always appears in the models, and while I have referred to it as the dove of Wisdom, it is also a Mercurius. Jung says the "white dove is another symbol of Mercurius who, in his volatile form of spiritus, is a parallel to the Holy Ghost." [11]

So Wisdom quite naturally sends her to the swordfish. The serpent, the dove, and the swordfish, united in the fate of the mermaid, all belong to Wisdom. They are the principle whose activity brings things to maturity and perfection.

When the mermaid asked for legs, it seemed to be a realization that if she is to get out of this deplorable condition, she must take the way she at first despised. This could be the way of sensation, for two legs would bring her onto the earth and in touch with life, and surely it is on the earth and in the humble place the self is born.

One must come to the fourth function to attain wholeness. It is verily the most touching task of analysis to rely on and educate this least used side of personality. In this position, the mermaid was able to admit it was mostly for herself. To attain wholeness is really for ourselves no matter whom it may affect in the long run, and only the honest approach brings co-operation from the unconscious.

It is important to know not only that one does something for oneself but also it must be recognized as for *the* self, that is, be-

[9] See Neumann, *Amor and Psyche*. See also Apuleius, *The Golden Ass*.
[10] See Jung, *The Spirit Mercurius*, for this theme.
[11] C. G. Jung, *Psychology and Alchemy*, page 416.

yond the narrow sense of ego. When one thinks it is done for another or for universal good, anima or animus devils will eat it up. The effects may go far beyond one, but the inner search is out of one's own need. Often it happens people are so caught by the new things they learn in the journey into the unconscious that they immediately want to give it to the world or make a system. It is natural but not wise, for it is easier to attempt to save others than oneself, and so put the problem of redemption outside. There is the story of an old woman who encountered a wise old woman in a lane. The old woman gave her a loaf of bread, and told her the recipe was imprinted on the base of the loaf. The woman was so thrilled she called a neighbor to taste it, and another and another. They thought it was excellent, and then the time came when they asked for more. The loaf had gone, and in her enthusiasm the woman had not studied the recipe. She could not reproduce the loaf and she could not find the wise old woman. Everyone had had a taste and no one had anything lasting. Had the woman baked one herself as the recipe suggested, she would have been able to distribute out of her personal labor, and even hand the recipe on, for the wise old woman must always disappear if she has not been made one's own. One is not related to the wise old woman, even if one has met her in a lane, without the labor she demands.

In the final portion of this chapter of the fantasy, there is a storm on the lake which becomes so full it forms a river that stretches to the sea. This depicts the path of faith that follows the sacrifice, for the river is the flow of life that ultimately joins the sea, the primordial womb from which, often in mythology, life began.

If we sum up the progress of the story to this point, we find that from a question asked of her creator, the mermaid has put herself into direct and meaningful contact with Him and Wisdom. These two with the aid of the Mercurius figures bring her into a realm of human realization and humanness. It seems important for these archetypes that she attain humanness, as if nature needs humanness for its own completion. The motifs used are those which, in mythology, have always led back to the beginnings, and so we see at once the fantasy is universal and non-personal.

When the mermaid found she was a woman, she realized she

must endure "the becoming." To become human could seem very ordinary but for it being the fate of God. It is the human who has the becoming eternally within, for to become a self one touches life. She had to come into the world as human, and says, "So this is death." That in one way is true, when the divine spark is fettered by the flesh, yet she is told that it is life. Here one could speak of it being the place of real human birth, the place of the soul's descent into the material world and human reality, to assume the burden and the suffering which are a condition of the soul's desire to know itself. In analysis it is a surrendering up of one's superior side, which is more divine and free, to be fettered by one's inferior side.

Finally, the age of the old man impressed the writer of the fantasy. He was so old he seemed like boundless time. In Mithraism it is stated that "Boundless Time," a god, embodied within himself the powers of all the gods.[12] The first emanation was Wisdom. The Hegelian idea was that the starting point of everything was in the thought as it existed in God, and the theory was derived from the idea of infinite time or, as they said, the personified Boundless Time as the ultimate fact in nature. These few examples are taken from the many which exist on the subject, and their connection with the fantasy needs no explaining. However, it is amplifications such as these which immediately bring a modern work into touch with ideas which have occupied the thought of man throughout the ages. The fantasy reveals that the unconscious is still in touch with the past and that he, man, modern man, is rooted in the ages. This method of using analogy demonstrates the existence of corresponding material, but the value does not lie in the discovery of these ancient ideas to add a sort of verifying factor. The importance lies in the recognition that basic principles have existed and still do exist, and this is the realization that enlarges consciousness and links one with life on a wider horizon. One sees in the unconscious not only one's own connections with things that have always been, but sees the path of developing consciousness and the history of mankind.

You will notice that this fantasy develops intensity and feeling as it progresses. One is aware of the feeling involvement of the

12 Franz Cumont, *Doctrine of Mithraic Mysteries*, pages 105ff.

writer. The mermaid begins to suffer human qualities. She is beset, the serpent warns her, by doubts "such as humans have." This is the human conditions, the suffering for which Wisdom bestows the heart she has "knitted" and into which she has given of herself. There is longing, aspiration, greed, contemplation, sacrifice. The greater the longing, the greater the sacrifice. This is the first great sacrifice which leads to rebirth and, as such, is surely the symbolic expression of a new beginning. So naturally the fantasy now leads down as well as up, for development of personality requires both.

CHAPTER **5**

The Myth with Commentary continued
(The Journey)

ONE DAY the woman came to the man and said, "Father, I must leave you and go my own way."

The old man looked up in surprise. "Are you not happy here in the castle? Have you not all you want?"

"Yes, I am happy here and I have all one could ask for one's enjoyment. Yet it is not all that I want, for my heart tells me there is much that I need yet to do."

"Then you do not love me sufficiently to stay?"

"I do love you. Yet me heart burns and I must tear myself from you. Do not think that it is easy for me. To break away from the comforting enfoldment of your arms is a torture I must bear."

"Then neither jewels nor riches will stay you, my child. Where will you go?"

"Where the road leads me."

"Then you will take with you my horse and my purse."

"No. I will take neither your purse nor your steed. I will take but my own simple gown, and will cast myself upon the hospitality of the world."

"The world is dangerous," he warned. "You have not known its dangers."

"Has the merest babe known its danger? Yet it wills to live. But there are dangers here, too, grave dangers. One cannot escape them, therefore I must go alone and unaided."

"But my worthy steed surely you will need."

"Many times, oh, many times, my father, yes, I will. Yet if I have not your steed, surely I will find myself another."

The old man groaned. "Then this you must take," he said. From a casket he took a golden heart studded with jewels and hung it about her neck. "Keep it always," he said. "This castle is the heart of your sacrifice. Take this as its symbol and let no man take it from you, even if you perish of hunger and thirst."

The woman took the jewel and prepared herself to leave the castle. She clung to the old man, then turned away to the trail that led she knew not where. As she walked along the road, she paused once to look back. The old man waved and she hesitated before she could go on. A cold fear gripped her, and a longing to stay. She put her fingers to her lips and blew him a kiss. Then she continued out of his sight.

The old man entered the castle and, kneeling before an altar, prayed: "Keeper of Destinies, though she walks through the valleys and ascends to the mountains, be her stay. Place Thy winged steed beneath her feet, and Thy sword in her right hand."

Then because his heart was breaking, he bowed his head into his hands. Wisdom came and touched him gently on the shoulder and he looked up.

"You have done well not to keep her," she said. "Woe unto the woman who refuses life and clings to her father . . . and woe and triumph to her who hath the courage to depart. Surely she will go into the dark places and surely she will need the sword of the Almighty One and His winged steed when her feet stumble along the byways."

"Yet if I could bring her back! Dark is the agony of suspense."

"Does not the mother of every child know that? Do you think that I, too, who gave her this heart, am not concerned?"

Out over the long trail the woman walked, drinking sometimes at a stream, pausing to watch children at play. For three days she went, passing by green fields and sleeping at night beneath the hedges, then into a valley where a little village lay.

Through the streets she went looking again and again at the faces about her, then she entered a market place where people sat eating and drinking. She leaned awhile against a pillar of stone, for she was tired and hungry, and as she watched them eat she grew more hungry. But how could she eat, she who had no money to buy? At a table near sat some men drinking wine and laughing with each other. She went forward, for she knew she had thrown herself upon the hospitality of the word.

"Who is the maiden?" cried one.

"Possibly a prostitute," replied another.

"She does not look like a prostitute," said a young man. "She is not beautiful but she has something in her eyes."

"Why," laughed the first, "do you not paint her? Are you not always looking for models?"

She joined them then, and said: "Gentlemen, I am hungry. Could you spare me some food?"

"Have you no money," asked the first, "that you should beg for food?"

"I have no money and I have come a long way."

"Where do you think we get our money? We earn it, and not to spend on thriftless beings. . . . But come sit here. Maybe we could give you a chance. What is that you wear about your neck?"

"The heart my father gave me."

"Let me look. It has five jewels. Sapphire, emerald, ruby, topaz, and a great white diamond in the center. Woman, you say you have no money, but you have more wealth than most of us. I will buy your jewel and then you can have enough money"—he paused to laugh—"yes, you will have enough money for all of us."

"Sell him your jewel," said a second. "He is a dealer and will give you a good price."

She put her hand about the heart as if to protect it. "I will never part with it," she cried. "It is the only thing I have in the world."

"Sheer sentiment," cried the dealer. "Many people sell me their jewels, though they do not want to part with them, but they have enough pride not to beg while there is an honest way."

The night was drawing in and she rose to leave them, and as she turned away she heard the dealer say: "It is a precious jewel . . . the impudence of the woman that she should beg. I will see more of her, for I like that jewel, and time will break her spirit."

Then as she disappeared, the young artist, who had been silent the while, rose up and took his hat. "He is going off to paint her image." said the dealer. "Sentiment and more sentiment."

As the evening closed into darkness, the woman wandered into an alley and, cold and hungry, she curled herself up in a doorway of a shop whose shutters were drawn and for whom the busy traffic of the day had ceased.

As she thought of the men she clung more closely to the jewel at her neck and, shivering a little, she rested her head upon the stone wall. From the shadows a woman spoke.

"Why do you come here? This place belongs to me."

"I will do no damage. All I need is to rest awhile."

"Where have you come from?"

"Across the mountains, three days. Tomorrow I can work that I might eat."

"You are hungry?"

"Terribly."

The strange woman paused. "Look, my place is just around the corner . . ."

"Isn't this your place?"

"Oh, this. Yes, this is my place too. . . . I wander around here at night. Give me your arm and I will help you to my room. At least I can offer you some food and a bed. That is not going to break me, but I must not stay long with you. . . . I must attend to my business. Don't look at me like that. I am a prostitute, but prostitutes have hearts, you know. I see by your fine linen you are a lady. It may be that you would not want help from me."

"Oh, I do. Indeed I do. It is the love, the love which counts."

"You don't seem a bad little thing, you know. Here we are. I will put some food out for you, run you a bath, and you can put yourself into that bed. I have another bedroom, so I will not disturb you. This soup will warm you, and I will take a cup with you before I leave. I know what it is to be hard up, you know. That is the reason why I came to be what I am. Amazing where your stomach leads you." She paused and looked at her guest seriously. "You are not really beautiful, you know, but there is something about you. . . . But listen, you *are* hard up, aren't you?"

"Yes, very. I have not so much as a penny piece."

"Yet there is a rare jewel at your neck. Did a man give it to you?"

"Yes. My father."

The prostitute threw back her head and laughed. "Oh, I was thinking in terms of a man friend. Do you have one?"

"No. I have never had one."

"Never?"

"Yes. Never."

"Then you don't know about life. Good heavens, there are more things in this world than one would dream about. Couldn't you sell the old man's trinket and keep going for a bit?"

"No, that I will never do. It is far too precious. I mean it has an intrinsic value."

"I know how you feel. Look, I will show you something." She opened a small box and drew out a thin gold ring. "This belonged to my mother. They took it from her finger when she died and gave it to me. There were times when I could have sold it for bread, but somehow I would rather have died . . . nearly did die a few times. So, you see, I know how you feel. I can guess your story. The old man died and that is all there is left. You hang onto it, girl, and things will come good. They have a habit of doing that. And you are welcome here until we get you going at something. But I must go now."

It was late that night before she returned to look in at the woman, who was sleeping soundly. Behind her stood a man. "Just take a peep at her," she whispered. "I do not know what we can get her to do unless she takes up my line. There is not much work going, and look at those hands. They have never done a scrap of work."

"It is she," replied the artist breathlessly.

"What do you mean by 'she'?"

"I saw her today. . . . Please do not let her slip away. I will be with you in the morning. I must paint her. . . . Heavens, what a painting it will make."

He came as he said, and offered the woman food and shelter if she would allow him to paint her. So he painted her once and again and again, for his pictures sold, and as he painted her he grew to love her. He grew accustomed to her being about the house, to seeing her in his garden, in his home and lying at his side with the moon streaming down upon her face. Hot burned his brushes upon the canvas and hot burned his kisses upon her face. "You are my inspiration," he would cry. "Never could I have painted this without you."

Then one evening he sat in the market place boasting, for his name was famous and people had come from afar to see and buy his art. "I have bought the most beautiful house in the city," he said. "I must have that which is suitable for her and for my work." And his eyes wandered after her as she talked and laughed with the women.

The next morning when she awakened, she found her jewel gone. Quickly she shook him from his slumber. "My jewel," she cried frantically, "oh, please hurry and help me find it."

The painter looked embarrassed. "I have to confess," he said, "I have sold your jewel. I had to have a large house for us, and the dealer offered me an absurdly good price. Think, it is better to have it in a home than hanging about your neck. Do not be upset. You will get used to being without it. Besides, you were always caring for it. Especially lately, as if you were always afraid of something happening. It is foolish to have something which causes you so much concern.

"You must go to the dealer and get it back," she cried.

"Don't be foolish. He will never give it back. He has been trying to get it for a log while. My darling, you must see it is the sensible way."

She stood as if transfixed. "You must go to your home alone, for I will not come with you. I cannot part with my jewel for worldly luxury. I must get it back."

"Please forgive me and do not leave me. . . . No, do not hurry to dress and leave. You cannot, you must not."

"I will."

"Your eyes burn with inward fire which is hurting me," he said sadly.

"My eyes will hurt you forever." Her voice was low and tremulous. "Have I not been for you an inspiration? Have I not stayed with you, slept at your side, entrusted myself entirely to you?"

"Of course. These things I could not deny."

"And it was you, whom I have loved, who has stolen my jewel. Oh, I do not blame you. You could not have known what it means. What you have done you have done, and it is I who have been the careless guardian. It is I alone who must get it back again."

The woman's first contact with a different world was with children and with nature, a naïve approach to the world and quite feminine. If we refer to the old man for a moment as the animus or the spirit, it is he who has now been left behind, and so quite rightly his horse and money are rejected, for they would represent masculine libido. While it is correct at this point to reject them, it is also true that spirit (Logos), the discriminating factor, is necessary for a woman's wholeness.

Once I was walking in a suburban village where there were very few people in the street at the time. A stranger, a woman, turned into the street and walked beside me. She said, as if we were the oldest of friends: "What sort of polish would you get for that floor? I don't want to put coverings down at this stage." I fell into the spirit of her relatedness and answered that I would use a certain type. She agreed, and went on to say that she did not like the house and could not settle in it, but since Charlie was working with a certain firm there was little she could do at the moment other than make as little effort toward permanency as possible. That I had never seen her before did not concern her, and that I did not know anything of the house or Charlie did not occur to her. She was an Eros creature related to everyone, and her business was naturally mine and of interest to me! It is the Logos side of woman that discriminates, divides, and marks off boundaries so that Eros does not flow into everything. Woman in an increasingly patriarchal society has had to develop the animus to exist. She is forced by the outside world to meet the demands made upon her. From the outside, man has demanded more than Eros from woman, he likes also the companionship and capacity of her intellectual animus to accompany him in his world. From inside it is the natural development of the woman's spirit, but where her Eros is undervalued either by man or herself, the animus develops in an effort to save her from nothingness. The woman I met was living in a world of unbounded Eros and with no Logos discrimination to guide her. The animus exists, of course, but in an undeveloped and diffused way.

To return to the fantasy, we encounter again the motif of

three days. If this leads to the fourth place or the fourth function, difficulties are to be expected, for it could lead her again into another place of suffering before wholeness could be attained. On the fourth day she reaches the village in a fatigued and hungry state. She has no money and no libido in this new world. She has to beg, yet begging is of little use where the hardest of work is demanded. She carries the jewel which, if traded for bread, would make her way in the world easy, but she cannot exchange this either for food or for the right to live there. "Sell your jewel and live at ease" is the wisdom of the world where ease and comfort are greater values than the inner riches that the jewel represents. It is true, one must sell something to live in this world. Where is one's debt, to the world or to the self? This is often the problem. Only if one can resist the peculiar and rational justice of the world can one serve the self. Here in the fantasy the woman is faced with rational justice; what right had she to live with them and retain the jewel? She had, however, just taken the journey along the way of nature and children who are not at one with the rational world. She drew away from the men's suggestion, for hers was an irrational journey where feeling (the heart which was now a principle more than an ego possession) was her evaluating guide. A place where collective demands were so strong made her afraid.

Her refusal brings her then to meet the prostitute, who is another side of Wisdom. She is an aspect of the self, who, because she is already more at home in reality and relatedness, can divulge a new way to her. In life it is the other unknown side of ourselves, often the unacceptable and despised, that contains the possibilities for transformation. By accepting the love and the help of this figure, she learned the prostitute owned a jewel which, even while she lived in the world, had not been traded for bread. Her jewel was a gold ring, a symbol of wholeness. She, like Wisdom, is an impersonal figure.[1] From the fact that Wisdom, the spouse of God, comes into the picture, her earthly aspect related to

---

[1] N.B. The Mother Goddesses are elemental beings, with unreflecting feminine reactions—the Mother Goddess acts right out of nature, with anger, cunning, etc., but at the same time she succors the suffering. Hers is a total reaction: charity, generosity, jealousy, vanity. She is the great whore who embraces all men.

man must surely constellate. She is the opposite, the one at home and related in Wisdom's natural creation. She is the otherness of Wisdom. Jung says: "The essence of the conscious mind is discrimination: it must, if it is to be aware of things, separate the opposites and it does this contra naturam. In nature the opposites seek one another—les extrêmes se touchent—and so it is in the unconscious and particularly in the archetype of unity, the self. Here as in the deity, the opposites cancel out, but as soon as the unconscious begins to manifest itself they split asunder, as at the Creation, for every act of dawning consciousness is a creative act, and it is from this psychological experience that all our cosmogonic symbols are derived." [2] In Active Imagination, symbols are chosen which convey certain, sometimes half realized, meaning. It is unlike the dream. However it is also true that in dreams, such a figure as we have now encountered can be an archetypal figure akin to Wisdom. To regard such a figure as representing the personal shadow would be to reduce its meaning and ultimate development. Moreover, it would require that Wisdom herself should be accepted on a personalistic level where she certainly does not belong. Wisdom and the prostitute are both extremely dynamic archetypal figures. The process of individuation does not begin on high but in dark unknown places, in the world below. It might be interesting at this point to refer to the Bible. In the Book of Proverbs one reads of the negative aspect of the feminine.

Say unto Wisdom thou art my sister; and call understanding thy
    Kinswoman:
That they may keep thee from the strange woman, from the
    stranger which flattereth with her words.[3]

This stranger is the one concerned with the wisdom of the world, its pursuits and pleasures, which have not always the hallmark of her opposite, Wisdom, her self whose praises are sung in Chapter 8. Psychologically, this one "subtle of heart" is the opposite aspect of Wisdom, who indeed makes choice necessary and conscious. As soon as man becomes conscious he is faced with

[2] C. G. Jung, *Psychology and Alchemy*, page 25.
[3] Proverbs 7:3, 4.

choice, and these two opposites demand the human equation, for in fact it is man's consciousness and choice that have split apart, and his psychological task is unification on a different level.

In analysis, the acceptance of the shadow is always a problem. This does not apply only to the personal shadow, for even more difficult can be the acceptance of the shadow of the self or the dark aspect of the Deity, or indeed, the opposite of Wisdom. Christianity has placed the whole of the darkness on man, so that when one like Job is faced with opposites in high places, certain values and ideals have to be sacrificed to greater understanding. Even though one should not dig too deeply into problems that remain unanswerable, in both the personal and archetypal realms it is acceptance and love of the shadow that have the transforming effect. Nature takes so much trouble with man, bringing him up against forces he has to transform. It was the prostitute who, understanding both worlds, understood also the woman's claim on both the world and the jewel. It was she, the shadow of the self, who led her to sleep in the world, and, after she had suffered, led her again to her jewel. Like Wisdom, she helps her and at the same time has a secret plot that inflicts suffering. In regard to her, Layard says: 'The prostitute is the archetype of the free woman untrammeled by man's law. For dreams are, on this level, the complementary opposite of life in the flesh. In external life she has to pay a price much heavier than that paid by the man, but in dreams she represents the bountiful earth mother, uncontaminated by thinking . . . who offers good things to all men and who is to be had for the asking. She is in fact the ultimate anima, the temple priestess who marries the god and bestows her favors upon devout men, thus raising them to a semi-divine status. On this spiritual level she is also Our Lady, who showers her gifts freely upon all men and who is profligate (note the word) with her divine favors. In fact she is in the psyche the virgin unspotted, pregnant with the boundless pregnancy of nature, translated into this spiritual sphere." [4] For woman, of course, she is not the ultimate anima but the ultimate self, for Our Lady is a symbol of individuation for woman. "A prostitute," continues Layard, "from the male

[4] See John Layard, *Eranos XIII. Incest Tabu and the Virgin Archetype*, pages 300ff.

point of view is a totally undifferentiated woman, just woman who will give what he wants on this undifferentiated level. Since differentiation is a thing that belongs to the conscious . . . this undifferentiation in the unconscious means for a woman freedom from the trammels of ego-consciousness and therefore the discovery of her true self." [5] Generally the prostitute carries a stigma in outer reality, but in the psyche represents reality on a different level. It is because she represents the freedom which is the essence of selfhood that in the world she is often the emotionally contaminated figure of rejection. When she is outside and can carry the rejection, one has no problem, but once she is discovered within, she is found to have a jewel and a meaning, as pointed out by Layard, which her transformation brings about. On this inner level she is a most dynamic figure.

The woman met her in her hour of need. In myths and fairy tales, once the hero has set out on a journey or a task, helpers appear. They are always those who know how things are from another side and, because they bring things that have been dark and unknown, they bring help. Appearing in the hour of need, she would be exceedingly welcome, and it is true, in extremity, one is humble enough to accept, so barriers against this otherness or shadow would not exist. She, the helper, embodies, a certain divine wisdom, and has access in the regions where the traveler has none. The prostitute, then, is the helper who appeared to the one who had heard the call from the inner world and responded. The woman was going, she had said, where the road would lead. It is when one really trusts oneself to life that such helpers appear. The prostitute as helper and companion adds the qualities required for wholeness. She helps to lead the initiate, but first she leads her into the world and sleep.

The Eleusinian Mysteries were said to have a transforming effect on the initiate, bringing him into closer relationship with the deity. One of the rites performed on the fourth day was the carrying of poppy seed, for it was said that poppy seeds were given to Demeter on her arrival in Greece to induce sleep. The initiate had to withstand demons and specters which depicted the difficulties besetting the soul in its approach to the gods, for man had fallen asleep in materiality and himself. Plotinus says that

[5] Ibid.

to be plunged into matter is to descend and then fall asleep, so man takes part in time and temporariness He slumbers in a sensuous world. It is then from this that the soul struggles to awake again. Psyche also fell asleep when she beheld corporeal beauty, and it was this final fall into the lure of matter that brought the aid of the god Eros, who, while he was thus brought into the realm of humanity, lifted her into the realm of the gods. The danger of sleep in the process of individuation is a widespread motif. In *Fragments of a Faith Forgotten* we read: "A youth went to a foreign land to retrieve the pearl from the serpent. There he met a youth fair and well favored:

And he came and attached himself to me,
And I made him my intimate,
A comrade with whom I shared my merchandise.
I warned him against Egyptians
And against consorting with the unclean;
I put on a garb like theirs
Lest they should insult me because I came from afar.
But in some way or other,
They perceived I was not their countryman:
So they dealt with me treacherously.
I forgot that I was the son of Kings,
And I served their King:
I forgot the pearl for which my parents had sent me.
And by reason of the burden . . . I lay asleep.[6]

The woman had separated from her creator and fallen asleep in the world. She had donned the dress of the community in which individual values did not count. The dealer, with the aid of the painter, secured the jewel. In this satanic role, he realizes the value, and, by taking it, awakens her from the inertia into which she had fallen. He is again a Mercurius figure, the dark god who intends consciousness. "Evil forceth men to prudence and preventeth them from falling asleep in indolent security." [7]

In life it is true that when one is not aware of what goes on in the unconscious, things will constellate outside, as if nature

[6] G. R. S. Mead, *Fragments of a Faith Forgotten*, The Robe of Light.
[7] Plotinus II:iii:18.

intended we should be more conscious and so provides the possibility in the form of the impact. In the fantasy, the painter points out that she *was* aware of the danger, for she was always concerned about the jewel. One is always concerned for that which one intuitively values and yet is not safely part of one. The woman's treasure was the jewel that was her own heart, her femininity, and the Eros principle. The old man had admonished her even if she died of hunger or thirst not to part with it. He who had given her life placed upon her a challenge also. Psychologically, femininity and the Eros principle are always challenged by the animus and the Logos world.

CHAPTER 6

The Myth with Commentary continued
(Tribulation)

SHE WENT first to the dealer. "What," he laughed, "you want to buy it back, and with what?"

"I will work," she said. "I will do anything. Do you not understand, I cannot let it go. My very life would go."

"Nothing you can offer would get it," he said. "The painter has been here before you and implored me for it, and because I do not trust the mood he is in I have hidden it in a place where none will find it or think to look. Woman, you are causing a lot of suffering to the man who saved you from starvation . . . you, an unknown stray. Why do you torment him? Women are heartless, selfish, and petty. It is a jewel for a queen, but not for such as you."

She went away then, and came to the home of the prostitute.

"I have come to you," she said, "because my jewel is gone and you had the wisdom to preserve the one your mother had." She told then to the prostitute the whole story, and her listener's eyes filled with tears.

"That is the trouble," she sighed, "with success. Once he would never have thought about that. I can give you a little money, but it would not buy the chain it hangs upon. Look, why don't you go home to your own country? You must surely have some relations there. This is no place for you. Here, take this money

and I will watch things for you here, and if there is any hope
of getting the jewel, I will."

The woman took the four coins in her hand and left; then as
she passed through the market place she saw some horses for sale.
She paused. If she could buy a horse it would make the journey
so much less difficult.

The dealer was there, and seeing her stand to consider, he
asked if she wanted to buy a horse.

"Yes, I do," she replied.

"And because I think it would be better for everyone if you
went on your way, I will sell you one. How much money have
you?"

"Four pieces."

"You can have that brown mare for four pieces." The men
standing around laughed. . . . "Oh, it will not travel far but it
will travel as far as you will go."

"But I will travel a long way."

Then there seemed to be some discussion in the group, and the
dealer came back to her and said:

"Perhaps I had better let you have the frisky silver horse in
my stables."

"I will take it."

"You will never ride it."

"I can but try."

"Well, I can afford to be generous. Give me your four pieces
and take the horse. Maybe you will not be able to ride it, but
that is your risk, and being honest, I have to let you know."

"I will take the risk," she replied, and the dealer, not a little
puzzled, went with her to the stables. When she looked up at the
horse her heart was afraid, and when she mounted it, it galloped
so swiftly away she had no time to look back at the dealer, who,
for a reason he did not know, took off his hat and watched until
she was far from sight. The last he had seen was a white speck
climbing quickly up the mountainside. "She is risking her life,"
he thought, "and I should not have done it."

In the valley the woman alighted to rest awhile and allow the
horse to drink at the stream. Then while she rested, to her surprise
the prostitute appeared. "How glad I am to find you," she said,

"I have so much to tell you, and I thought my horse would never overtake yours. Your jewel is safe."

"Safe! Oh, my friend, where?"

"Strangely it is within the horse you ride."

"But how could that be?"

"I will tell you. The dealer's stable boy comes to see me. They tell me things, you know. Sometimes when they have troubles, they like to talk about them; it seems to help. Anyway, he told me that the dealer had placed a small parcel in the chaff bin, and instructed the boy not to use chaff from there and to keep the place locked. But the boy forgot, and in the chaff was an apple that he unwrapped and gave to your horse, who loves to eat apples and carrots. When he realized what he'd done he replaced the apple with another one, but he was very worried and concerned lest the other contained a poison. However, I realized what must be in it."

"But it may not have been this horse who ate it."

"Yes, it was. That was the point. So when you went to buy a horse they were going to sell you the brown one. The only thing I could think to do was to get them to sell you the silver gray. It has given a lot of trouble, and the stable boy is the only person who has been able to ride him. Thus, while you were occupied with the others I slipped to the dealer and pretended to be jealous of you. I said, "Give her the silver; it will throw her and return, so you will get it back again.""

"You did this for me. Oh, how can I thank you?"

"You don't have to thank me. If the stable boy had not told me his worries I could have done nothing. Now it is your problem to get your jewel. You have to kill the horse."

"I could not do that."

"That is up to you. I imagine it may kill him anyway. Those well-bred horses are delicate. Somehow it seems to be his fate to be caught into this drama. But I must leave you. I hope you arrive safely, and someday perhaps you will come to see me again."

"Indeed I will."

After the prostitute had gone, the woman her her arms about the neck of the horse. "We will find a way," she whispered. "There must surely be a way, an easier way than death."

They rode on the next day and the woman thought constantly

of her jewel. She searched in the waste, but it had not passed from the horse, and her anxiety grew. "There must be an easy way," she thought, "and when I arrive home, my father will help me."

That day they were coming nearer the castle and the woman's heart leaped with joy, but when she dismounted, the horse would not drink. He seemed restless and irritated, and suddenly he broke into a wild gallop, circling madly up and down, and then racing wildly away from her and tossing his mane and whinnying. She was seized with terror and more terror until he had gone from her sight completely. And she, too, began to run wildly, whither she did not know. . . . Then, exhausted, she stood upon a rocky height trying to see him, and the horse came down the track below, enjoying his freedom and the winds that tossed his mane. How could she get to him? In her desperation, the woman took up a stone and threw it, and before her eyes the horse dropped to the ground, struck by the stone upon its temple.

With panting heart, she descended. There it lay, dead. There was agony then—suffering for the horse she had grown to love and grieving for her own predicament. Her jewel lay within the horse. She wrung her hands together. That night she slept with her head upon the horse. She had looked at the knife several times but did not dare to use it. There was sacrilege in it, it seemed, to cut even the lifeless form of the silver animal.

But on the following day, with tears streaming from her eyes, she gently opened the horse's side, piercing deeper and deeper. Into the wound she plunged her hand, her whole being revolted at what she did. Then at last, nauseated and ill, she drew forth the jewel. Then she knelt and kissed the brow of the horse several times, and brought branches of trees and placed them above him, and with slow step she set off for the castle.

There, her father seeing her coming in the distance came to meet her.

"My child," he cried. And she fell into his arms. "My child, you have returned."

"Yes, I have returned." She held out the jewel. "This I bring back to you. My poor heart I had given to another, but this heart which encompasseth us both I bring back."

"That is well done," said the old man.

"No, no. It is not well done. I have been a poor but earnest guardian. In joy I became careless, in sorrow distraught. And blood is on my hands, for I have slain with them the horse that bore me out of my travail, the horse I loved."

The man took her by the shoulders and turned her around. "Look," he said, "do you see who comes?"

"It is Wisdom. She does not change."

"Yes, it is Wisdom and she leads your horse. Maybe he will journey not quite so swiftly again. He too had to learn to obey."

"He was forced to carry that which should have been my burden only. But he is recovered. Oh, I know it, yes I know it. This is the work of Wisdom who made my own heart."

When Wisdom joined them she said, "This was my horse which I left in the village; because you could accept him, ride him, and overcome him, I now give him to you to whom he belongs."

Since the woman had lost her jewel, she realized she was the one responsible for retrieving it. She had been torn in conflict between the world and the jewel and so came again to another place of sacrifice and loneliness. No one can carry our burden for us. Quite naturally, she turned to the prostitute for advice, for she had kept protected her own gold ring. She needed reinforcement from the feminine side where she had been careless of values. To come again to the shadow is union with the self, for without the shadow one has no foothold in reality.

The modern woman is the product of a patriarchal society whose laws are of Logos and not of the heart; a society in which woman was condemned to be not herself but the masculine idea of woman, a condition sponsored and nurtured by her own animus. If an attempt is made by Logos to remodel Eros in his own image, feminine values fall into the limbo of the lost, and real feminine values look too much like nature with all its mysterious irrationalities and its dark forces. To find wholeness, one has to turn again to that which has been rejected, to the shadow where this other side is hidden, for one requires the instinctive forces which bind one to nature or things are too far up in the air. And for woman, that means possession by the animus, while for man it means the loss of his soul. It is the nature side from which woman learns real feminine values; neither Logos nor man can teach her that. In life, one so often finds that a man tries to remake his wife into his idea of the feminine rather than accept her as she is, not realizing he is losing her precious reality in an illusion.[1] Then one day a woman will wake up to the fact that she has lived out his ideas and not been true to herself. At that moment, she realizes an important thing: her jewel of uniqueness has been stolen, traded by the one she trusted to a dealer. The individual possession has been traded on a collective market. Then of course, if she sets out to redeem her treasure and become who she is, which is the fate bestowed upon her by her creator, she is not comfortable to live with any more and the husband fails to understand unless his own soul has called for his response. If this happens, they have a chance to relate again. The responsibility rests largely on the woman, for hers is an Eros relating role in its own right. The problem of the feminine role extends far into life. If the archetypal background of femininity is not understood at least feelingly or intuitively, outer values can be misused. Even the woman herself can see femininity from a masculine point of view and become a compulsive feminine under the aegis of her own animus. A sexuality ensues which is predominantly masculine in attitude and often passed off as the passionate nature of woman, whereas it is the realm of frigidity and its consequent desire. If a man has the gift of accepting the feminine with its waxing and waning moon qualities, he not only helps relatedness but his own soul, so that these values are not traded by him to a dealer, that is, to masculine ideas. Eros itself is a spirit, a gift of the feminine side of God. Sex without Eros is void of its real archetypal values, and life without Eros is unbearable. When man demands from a woman an animus reaction to life, that is, the acceptance of masculine values, he then becomes afraid of the very thing he has helped to produce. The woman's masculine side is then her governing principle and becomes his enemy in the realm of the masculine. He then is forced into more and more femininity, into reactions from his unknown feminine side, the anima. Here on

---

[1] The same ensues when a woman insists her idea of man be lived by the husband. Here a man sacrifices his values, is lost as a real male creature, or has to attempt a masculinity that is inadequate. To get to know his anima lessens such domination from the outside.

this level he contacts not real Eros, but negative femininity, which can devour his whole life.

Now in the fantasy the painter wanted to help, but his help, not being of the right kind, was rejected. He had created a second paradise from which she had to be expelled lest the dark rapture of the world become too alluring, yet it is as if one must "eat of the tree." The painter, of course, in taking the jewel, had aided in her expulsion from this second paradise. Once again the way is via the shadow, who knew the secret means and was unafraid subtly to outwit the dealer to give her help. In analysis, it is also true that a woman finds she has to be quick and cunning to outwit her own negative animus. The woman exchanges with the dealer four pieces for a silver horse. Worldly libido is exchanged for something more living and personal, and the silver horse could, in this case, refer to intuition.[2]

The dealer was the one who recognized the values, and while he has the sinister aspect of "robber," he is also "guide." She was robbed while she was asleep in her earthly paradise where everything seemed safe. In analysis it often happens that one is inclined to think one has arrived when, in fact, intuition has seized on ultimate things; or, having made certain progress one drops to sleep in a false paradise. In the dealer we see also the Trickster motif.[3] He has a tendency toward slyness and trickery, and on the other hand leaves himself open to be outwitted. He is a savior figure and an inflicter of suffering; a wounder who heals. The painter with his charm is another aspect of the Trickster, for the devil charms and hence his power. They are the dubious side of a trinity composed of the old man, dealer, and painter. This dealer is another Mercurius figure. As serpent, he was less differentiated corresponding to the less differentiated woman as mermaid. This dealer would be the one whom Jung has shown throughout his writings as Mercurius.

Mercurius, as an embodiment of the unconscious, is the spirit

---

[2] N.B. I want to avoid mixing the issue here, but the silver horse is also a close relation to Mercurius—to quicksilver whose philosophical meaning is the "spiritus vitae."

[3] Paul Radin: see *The Trickster* for reference on this motif.

which surpasses personality. He is the impulse from inner reality or underneath which rises from these depths of the body toward the spiritual sphere. He is the urge in the unconscious which co-ordinates diverse values and enlarges consciousness. He is a principle which assembles separate parts into a whole and so is the principle of individuation. Of him Jung says: "He is the spirit that penetrates into the depths of the material world and transforms it." [4] He is also identical with Nous. "Mercurius . . . is the world soul imprisoned in matter and, like the Original Man who fell into the embrace of Physis, is in need of salvation through the labors of the artifex. Mercurius is set free ('loosed') and re deemed." [5] In alchemy, the transforming substance is commonly identified as Mercurius, which chemically means quicksilver and philosophically is the spiritus vitae or world soul.[6] He says further in speaking of the origin of the medieval Mercurius: "Mercurius, however, had many things in common with the devil. . . . It is of the essence of the transforming substance to be on the one hand extremely common, even contemptible (this is expressed in the series of attributes it shares with the devil such as serpent, dragon, raven, lion, basilisk, and eagle), but on the other hand to mean something of great value, not to say divine. For the transformation leads from the depths to the heights, from the bestially archaic and infantile to the mystical homo maximus." [7] And Dr. Marie-Louise von Franz has said: "Mercurius is a divine mirror image of Christ within the chthonic sphere. He is another image of the self, displaying those dark uncertain ambiguous qualities of the self apparent often in the dreams of modern people. Hence so many tales featuring a Mercurius figure say that it should first be redeemed. He answers the modern need for a symbol that embraces more of the underworld, including more of the dark primitive impulses than the symbol of Christ in Church tradition accords." [8]

The god, the old man, was aware of his dark side as shown by

[4] C. G. Jung, *Psychology and Religion: West and East*, page 233.
[5] Ibid., page 277.
[6] C. G. Jung, *Psychology and Alchemy*, page 126.
[7] Ibid., page 128.
[8] *Archetypal Patterns in Fairy Tales*, page 69.

his concern when the woman left the castle. When he appears so thoroughly good and solicitous it is necessary to be wary; the opposite is lurking. Hence it is a natural enantiodromia that she meets the dealer who steals the jewel. The good old man bestows the jewel and his shadow takes it away. The connection of these two is obvious by their mutual concern for the treasure. The old man's shadow side, once she has fallen from grace, instigates the means for her spiritual renewal. The one who ultimately outwitted the dealer was Wisdom's shadow. In both cases the shadow was the instrument of redemption. To cope with the dealer, his own methods were used. This is necessary when coping with the dark side. The woman accepted the wisdom of the shadow who was competent to deal with that side of the situation. If one does not know the shadow in life, one is incompetent to deal with facts on this level. However, as trickster or the dark side of the old man, the dealer really wanted to be cheated. The risks he took forced the woman to take risks also. His transformation began when he removed his hat and reflected on his actions. Without reflection, consciousness is not possible.

The jewel by strange chance was in the horse. The jewel is often cognized and carried along by intuition, but for it to remain forever in the realm of intuition would mean it would never be an experience. So this precious function has to be painfully over-thrown. The overthrowing of the superior function is like death, like the slaughtering of one's most vital being. But the woman is helped all through by one who is in touch with reality. Because she is an archetype, she can point a way which is painful on the human level. She is the great Nature Mother who demands sub-mission. In order to individuate, a woman is always faced with submission to the Great Mother, while for a man the necessity is to overcome her. Here the modern woman is faced with a great difficulty, for the spirit or animus is highly developed. So it always follows that when a woman is faced with submission to the Great Mother it is always linked with the transformation of the animus. She is forced to fight against his negative demands and so with every conflict earns a little more of his redemption as well as her own renewal. Again and again she comes to the place of sub-mission to the feminine, but it is a special submission, for she, too, must disobey the devouring mother, that is, the negative aspect of the mother archetype. When negative things oppose one, they at the same time liberate one. They are in themselves an incentive, for only by collision with life does one know that one lives. Overindulgent parents save from pain only to inflict a greater pain, that of non-living. Existence of mankind means suffering, therefore the dark side of the old man is forced to persecute the woman in order that she will seek her wholeness. Through this act he becomes the whole god, the double aspect, in order that she will become whole woman. The redemption of man is the redemption of God.

Wisdom had left the horse in the village; he represents earthly libido and power, but he is also extrasensory perception. Intuitions which control us are not possessed by us, and the prostitute knew something of this when she said it was his fate to be caught into the drama, and so does the woman when she says, "He was forced to carry that which was my burden." It must be the burden of the whole being to individuate. We cannot leave responsibility for the care of the jewel to others or to the Church. It is also true that when one is unconscious, the animal side can run off with the treasure. In Indian philosophy, the horse has been called a symbol of the whole world, and in this fantasy the woman was leaving behind the world in which she had "fallen asleep."

Here we arrive at the motif of sacrifice again. The second sacrifice: it is a return to other values. So much had she gained in humanness that she found it difficult to sacrifice the horse until he forced her action by getting her into a frenzied state. In this second sacrifice, she was more aware than in the first, for she knew she sought to regain her treasure, but she could not accomplish her mission without his help. This is also the sacrifice of life impulse, the sex impulse, intuition, etc., and is a surrendering to the transpersonal life.

Wisdom, we are told, had placed the horse in readiness. She is always behind things, and the right attitude brings about her activity. Wisdom said that, because she had overcome him, he was hers. The woman had sacrificed animal libido connected with the world, but now knew that libido itself was the gift of wisdom and could not die. Only by recognizing our gifts are from the gods are we safe from inflation, but having received the gifts, we must learn to control them or we will be possessed blindly.

Earlier the woman had refused the father's horse—the way of masculine libido—to deal with the world. Through hardship and suffering she then receives as her own the horse of Wisdom, the feminine principle. To accept the masculine way removes a woman from real life; to come again to the establishment of feminine values in a modern world means hardship, suffering, and sacrifices.

At the risk of putting in too many quotations, I cannot leave this portion of the work without including what Jung says in his discussion of the type problem in poetry. "Spitteler's Prometheus, like his God, turns away from the world, the periphery, and gazes inwards to the middle point, that 'narrow passage' of rebirth. This concentration, or introversion, brings the libido gradually into the unconscious, whereby the activity of the unconscious contents is increased—the soul begins to 'work' and creates a product which tends to emerge from the unconscious into consciousness. The conscious, however, has two attitudes—the Promethean, which withdraws the libido from the world, introverting without giving out, and the Epimethean, which is constantly responding in a soulless fashion, held by the claims of external objects. When Pandora makes her gift to the world it means, psychologically, that an unconscious product of great value is on the point of reaching extraverted consciousness, i.e., it is seeking a relation to the real world. Although the Promethean side, i.e., the artist, intuitively apprehends the great value of the work, his personal relations to the world are so subordinated to the tyranny of tradition that the work is merely appreciated as a work of art and not at its real significance, viz., as a symbol that promises a renewal of life. In order to convert it from a purely aesthetic interest into a living reality, it must also reach life, and be accepted and lived in the sphere of reality. But if the attitude is mainly introverted and given to abstraction, the extraverted function is inferior and is therefore under the spell of collective restrictiveness. This restrictiveness prevents the soul-created symbol from living. Thus the jewel gets lost; but one cannot really live if 'God,' i.e., the highest symbolic expression of living value, cannot also become a living fact. Hence the loss of the jewel also signified the beginning of Epimetheus' downfall.

"And now the enantiodromia begins. Instead of taking for

granted, as every rationalist and optimist is inclined to do, that a good state will be followed by a better, since everything tends toward 'upward development,' the man of blameless conscience and universally acknowledged moral principles makes a compact with Behemoth and his evil host, and even the divine children entrusted to his care are bartered to the devil.

"Psychologically, this means that the collective, undifferentiated attitude to the world stifles man's highest values; it thus becomes a destructive power, whose influence multiplies until a point is reached when the Promethean side, namely the ideal and abstract attitude, places itself at the service of the soul, and, like a true Prometheus, kindles for the world a new fire." [9]

The jewel in our fantasy is feminine value, which needs to be placed at the "service of the soul." It touches the deep problem of modern woman which must be brought out and told, for woman herself has allowed divine feminine values to be "bartered to the devil." A new value rises, a new readiness accompanies it, according to such documents of the unconscious. In life women mainly blame men for the theft of the jewel. But they themselves swallow traditional thinking and don't smell the anti-Eros aroma in it. Much the same way as Adam did not stand by his Logos principle and reject the temptation of the woman, does the woman neglect to realize her principle and protect it. This protection does not mean an attack on Logos, or man, but a deeply sincere attitude giving value to the Eros principle so that it stands in proper relation to Logos. They are the two columns of creation, a divine Syzygy which stand together on the foundations of Ethos.

The idea of such balance can be found in a saying attributed to Jesus: "Being asked when His Kingdom would come He replied: 'When two shall be one, that which is without as that which is within, and the male with the female, neither male nor female.' . . . Locke says the passage 'seems too riddling to be quite in accordance with the Master.' " [10] A similar thought is expressed in the writings according to Thomas discovered in papyrus form in 1945 near Nag Hamâde.[11] One can accept that such a saying

[9] Jung, *Psychological Types*, page 227-29.
[10] Roderic Dunkerley, *The Unwritten Gospel*, page 121.
[11] Gospel According to Thomas, page 57.

would seem puzzling as Locke has declared. Yet, with the findings of analytical psychology, the inner meaning of such sayings attributed to Jesus becomes clarified.

Another interesting passage from the *Martyrdom of Peter* [12] is the following: "Except ye make the right hand as the left hand and the left hand as the right hand, and that which is upwards as that which is downwards, that which is before as that which is behind, ye shall not know the Kingdom of God."

[12] Dodd, page 89.

CHAPTER 7

The Myth with Commentary continued
(The Attainment)

THE WOMAN was much alone and this she thought: "We both live in my heart at the moment, but we must be together in his heart also."

And because she saw no way to get close to him, really to understand and be understood, she asked the boy who attended the old man to let her take his place. To this he agreed on one condition, that she should cut off her hair and give it to him. Reluctantly she cut off her tresses and handed them to him in exchange for his clothes, and then she proceeded to tend the old man, hoping thus to get to know him more closely.

The old man recognized her and his eyes filled with sadness and he attempted to remonstrate with her, but she put her fingers to his lips and said, "It is well for me to tend you. Surely I am the child of your grief and not your flesh. Who else could care more? And if I cannot bear to be separate from you, how is it you can bear to be separate from me?"

"And you have sacrificed your lovely hair to be near me," the old man said.

"Did I not sacrifice my heart that you might live and not be sad? But what have you sacrificed since those first tears?"

"Do you demand of me also a sacrifice?"

"Exactly. Sacrifice your heart that you will know also that you live. You can make sacrifice upon your altar, but in that you have not sacrificed yourself."

"It seems you are as Eve."

"But you are not yet Adam."

"He came out of his Paradise."

"And you are out but you do not know it. If one lives there is no Paradise, yet the gateway is the same both for the coming and going."

"Hath not the spirit of darkness claimed you?"

"I am beyond distinguishing."

"I will go away," he said quietly.

"Yet when I went, you asked me if I did or did not love you sufficiently to remain. Today when I know, you are prepared to leave me."

"Something in me wants that I should remain for you what I am. It is not easy but it is so." He kissed her on the forehead. "It is a pity you could not have remained a child."

"But," she cried, "I was born a woman."

The old man prepared for himself a few articles of clothing and made his departure from the castle. He did not stop to look back but strode forth over the mountains.

The woman was sad but she did not attempt to stay him. Then as the days passed she grew afraid, and mounted her horse and went to find her friend the prostitute, who flung open the door and welcomed her warmly.

"But you are sad," she said, "so very sad. Tell me what is troubling you."

The woman told her whole story and what she had done, and the prostitute said, "You love him and why not?"

"He seemed so near and so far away, and I must get him back from afar. I have tried to draw him near, but my way is not his way. Whom else could I love?"

The prostitute looked at her thoughtfully. "You know," she said, "you have made one sacrifice after another, but are you willing to sacrifice your pride?"

"Surely I have already sacrificed it."

"No, not really. It is one thing to push a man into realizing you are a woman, and another just to drop your pride and place yourself in his way without pushing the responsibility or burden onto him. That is what we all want to do—go so far and leave the burden to the man."

"But that is not my way."

"And why?"

"I do not know."

"I do. It is pride. It is just the fine subtle margin in the way we do things."

"Oh, but I could not. He might hate me. I could not bear his anger."

"You speak as if he were more than human, for what is a trifle of human anger but a stimulant?"

"Oh, he is more than human. He is God. Yet if I take your advice it is because I must. He is so close and so far. That is the conflict. He is father but more than father. He cannot really live for me unless I draw him close. He may as well be that stone image, unless he also feels near. One cannot live like that. You are right. One must risk fire, risk mistakes, risk even death, else how do you know life from death?"

"Where will you find him?" asked the prostitute gently.

"He will have gone to the mountain Donna Buang, on the top of which is a cottage overlooking a valley. That is where I will find him."

"Then you must take my red gown, it is warmer than yours, and, look, I have here my mother's wedding ring to place on your hand. I have never wanted to put it on anyone before, and certainly not myself. But there is something sacred in what you do, more sacred than any marriage. I do not understand, but there it is."

Once upon the road the woman turned her horse toward Donna Buang, and as it climbed the circling road of the mountain she felt weak, ill, and afraid. It was as if the fire which burned in her so fiercely turned deadly cold. She wanted to turn back. Twice she paused before she could continue. Then she saw the gold ring upon her hand and thought of the prostitute's trust in her, and she went timidly on.

At the door of the cottage she paused; then, as there was no sound, she let herself in. It was cold and uninhabited. There was no sign that he had been there. Disappointed and relieved, she went to the horse and put him warmly in a stall. Then she returned and drew the curtains from the window and looked out. Long white clouds wisped down upon the lake in the valley, caressing it with loving fingers, with tendrils that united heaven and earth. She sighed and turned away, and wearily threw herself upon the bed to rest.

Back at the castle the old man had returned. For days he had fought within himself, and now by impulse he found his way back. Only the serving boy was there, and he asked where the woman had gone. He replied he would tell him only at a price, and the price he asked was that the old man should give him his beard. The old man was enraged, caught the boy, threatened him, and kicked him soundly. The boy was adamant. Then because he was desperate, the old man handed him the scissors with bad grace and the boy cut away his beard and shaved his face clean. Then he gathered up the long beard and left the man standing before the mirror, looking at himself as if he had never seen himself before. "How shall I know now," he cried, "that I am wise? Surely this beard was the sign of my wisdom."

"I only am wise," said Wisdom, standing at his side. "That beard separated you from the world. Yes, the boy has done well."

Then suddenly the man remembered and said, "He has not told me where she is."

The boy returned and directed him to visit the prostitute, then, taking a belt from his waist, he gave it to him saying, "I made it from her hair. It may be good that you wear it."

The old man took it and saw it was finely woven of her golden hair, and reverently he placed it about his waist. "I am sorry I was so angry with you," he said. "I apologize."

The boy's eyes smiled. "There is no need, sir, for I enjoyed it. It was the first time I had seen you really human."

"Who are you, boy?"

"Me? Oh, I am Humble. It is the lot of most people to have known me sometime in life. It is my lot to be humble always. People are mostly like you, sir, they kick me when I make demands."

The man's eyes twinkled and he stroked his chin caressingly. "One of your children, Wisdom," he said.

"They are all mine," she replied. "The wise and the foolish, the bad and the good, the arrogant and the humble. They find for themselves who they are."

The man went his way then, and when he arrived at the prostitute's home and she opened the door, he spoke without introductory remark. "Is my child here?"

"Your child? . . . Oh, please come in." She invited him to sit. "Yes, I am her friend. But surely you are not her father."

"Yes, I am. . . . Tell me, is she here?"

"But you see, I must be sure before I let anyone see her. She is not happy and I could not have her annoyed. You will pardon me, but she speaks of you as if you were the oldest and most distant man in the world."

"I believe I am."

The prostitute shook her head. "Then I will give you some nourishment, for you have a fair distance to travel. Here, drink this and listen. She is clad in a dark red gown and has set off on her silver horse to reach a cottage on Mount Donna Buang, which lies beyond the Bulla Road."

"Why would she go there?"

The prostitute turned away, but she was watching him closely. "I believe she could think of nothing further. When her heart aches, you like to get far away. When you have thought and thought you can't think any more, you seek a retreat. It may be that is why she has gone there."

"Thank you. I will follow her," he said, and he, too, took the winding trail up Donna Buang.

It was past nightfall when he arrived, and when he entered the cottage there was no sound but the woman's measured breathing. The man walked over and looked down at her lying there in the moonlight. Her short hair tumbled down about the pillow. He touched it with his fingers and then placed his hand upon the hair belt at his waist. Then he placed his hands under her shoulders and drew her to him, murmuring, "Thank heaven you are safe and I have found you."

Out of her half dream she placed her hands upon his shoulder and drew his lips to hers. "I knew," she whispered, "that if I could really know you, you would be like this."

They had found each other, and it did not matter that a storm broke over the mountains. Their words were for each other and not to be shared even with the silence of the night.

"You have brought me to life," he said.

"We are fate for each other," she replied, "and how could I love you completely while you were so far away? I had to risk that I lose you completely in order to find you. Yet do not think I have not and do not fear your nearness. I now know that I am meant, that I have a purpose and not only an existence. You were my God standing on the edge of infinity and now you are my God near at hand."

"You asked me that I should sacrifice also my heart. How could I since you are my heart . . . you are my soul. This I could not sacrifice."

"I know it now. Once I did not understand."

"My heart struggled within me, that she might be realized."

"And realize," she added. "You asked me once if I did not love you sufficiently to stay. One has to go out in order to return."

"I, too, know that now. Pride wanted that I should remain the great wise one for you."

She looked up. "Is not nearness and understanding the greatness? Who can measure something which is in the distance?"

The Love Song of the Becoming

Woman: For me thou art the sun of my being, and for thee I am the earth, the dark earth and mysterious. To you I cry to ravish me with the joy of your love. Seek me out and fructify the earth of my being, that through thy light I may bring forth fruit. Warm is thy breath, as the tropical breeze. Fiery as the furnace which blasts the desert, and gentle as the zephyr which brings to the evening rest. Strong is thine arm extending into the heavens. Who could stay thy might or turn away from thy demands? Tell me, that I may bring forth and sing a hymn of my receiving.

Man: Thou art surely the dark, mysterious earth. Thy breasts as the mountains which feed the sea, the forests and the fruit thereof for which thy body is the living stream. Woman, thou conceivest in dark mystery wherein thou art both sacred and profane. Thou art the earth, my soul.

Woman: And when thou committest to be brought forth thou art dark and unknowing. Thou art the spirit of the universe . . . urging, ever urging to he light, that thou mayest know thy seed which the earth bears for thee.

In the morning the woman watched the clouds rise from the lake wisping ever upward to the heavens. As they had lain cradled in the lake, so her love had lain close to her heart, and as they had risen to move far off, never to return to this spot again—for the nature of things was the eternal return but never the same, for it is also the becoming—surely this was her sacrifice also. She knew she could not claim him forever. "What right have I to the father?" she cried. "Every right and no right. Yet no one can ever give up what one has found. I cannot sacrifice," she cried, "and yet I cannot look upon his face."

Then looking up, she saw Wisdom and she held out her arms. "Wisdom, help me to understand, in the hour of my greatest joy comes my greatest sorrow. Must they ever go hand in hand?"

"You are right that you cannot look upon his face. You have sought the highest joy and knowledge and the price must be sacrifice."

"Is it that I dream that the sun shines upon the earth and blesses it? Is it a dream that I am pregnant with the spirit of him who gave me life? Is it true that I dwell for ever in the bosom of my father? I feel too weak to be alone."

"You will not be alone. You will bring forth again and again, and nature will be your companion. Even as the trees shed their leaves and their fruit for the renewal, so will be your way. If it were not so, the stream of life would dry up. Nothing is your own. Neither your possession nor the breath of life. In what you bring forth you will have his image and his spirit."

"Yet even that is not my own."

"Not even that. Who can possess another when all is possessed in one? As the waters flow from the mountains to the sea, as they are lifted up again and poured forth, neither the skies nor the mountains nor the sea possess them forever. Things are always there yet everchanging. That which brought them forth changes not that they might return. The pattern is the same though the seeming changes."

Her return to the castle meant for the woman a change of attitude toward the old man, and she wanted to bring about a change in him. In analysis it is found that as one's attitude to and understanding of the archetypes change, it brings about a change in the archetypes themselves. The unconscious begins to turn toward us the face we turn to it. It takes patience and endurance and indeed a great love to await the change.

In order to make some progress, the woman seeks the aid of the boy who demands her hair. She resorts to a feminine faculty to evaluate the means by the end. Some of the dark and devious methods used toward her had redeemed her and also brought her a little lower down. She had gradually been pushed out of the realm of the gods to become more human. She discovered there was a more subtle means than direct approach, and she began to use a moonlight consciousness rather than the sun of day. You will recall that as "mermaid" she was unconscious or partly conscious femininity. A woman who functions mainly on her Logos or masculine side, however resplendent that might be, is as unconscious in the Eros or feminine realm as a man more naturally is. So the lowering was the lowering of Logos standards to allow Eros more development. Though she asks a sacrifice from the man also, she does not rob him. She seeks a way without violating his independence. To confront and oppose the masculine principle, to dominate it, would bring disaster. Eros seeks yet another way which the more earthly sister and the boy could reveal to her.

However, before anything can be accomplished she must give up her hair. Hair which springs from the head usually symbolizes thoughts. Her thoughts (Logos) had been too active and had to be sacrificed to the boy who is an Eros figure. We can see from his activity of relating the man and the woman that he is Eros, so possibly it was animus or Logos thoughts that he demanded as a sacrifice, which is quite a reasonable demand in the realm of Eros.

Later, this hair was given to the old man. In folklore it is rather a general principle that he who receives a piece of hair has power over the individual, or at least some connection with him. In one story, Achilles kept his hair uncut because his father, Pelius, had vowed it to the river Spercheius. It was the custom to offer the hair to the local river, and Achilles left home as a boy so his hair could not be cut while he was under the vow. As this fantasy now enters the realm of the incest taboo, it may not be going too far to suggest the cutting of the hair was only possible after her inner readiness to break that taboo which had driven her from the castle. The incest taboo itself has to do with childhood and security. It is as old as consciousness and practiced by primitive tribes. It was this taboo which forced people out into the world. There is always a natural yearning for return; it is a search for divine peace. Christianity has put the goal of ultimate unity with the creator into the hereafter. This yearning back to the beginnings would be quite misunderstood as sexual desire. On a spiritual level only is the breaking of the taboo legitimate, that is, as the spiritual union with God. In life and in the fleshly realm it is quite rightly opposed by society. The idea of union, unio mystica, is not sex sublimated into spiritual existence; it is an innate spiritual demand. On the chthonic level the desire can be misunderstood and manifest as sexual desire on the physical incest level. Behind this misconception is an archetypal pattern, which, when understood, puts the desire into the right realm. Human beings are forced out of original unity into consciousness, and somewhere there is always a natural yearning back to a state beyond consciousness or conflict, in the bosom of the creator. The search for the deity is an archetype universally existent in mankind. It is called forth by the great power of the ultimate conjunction, the power of which can be seen running right through the created world.

There is a great danger in being contained in an unconscious state, and it is also a danger and suffering to break from it, but only this way can real union take place. The boy who is an Eros figure is the one who can relate the two again. He was the god who entered the human realm to lift the status of Psyche, and in this case uses the hair as a link or medium. The hair was in ancient times a medium of connection or union. One dedicated a lock of hair to God, thus putting onself in communion with

God. The boy Eros transferred the woman's hair over to the man. First he cut the hair, and it is an interesting fact that in 470 B.C., to wear the hair short denoted one was not free, so he, as Eros, had to do away with the flowing hair that was a sign of freedom. She was now more and more under the principle of Eros. One severs connection with nature as one becomes conscious, as suggested by the long hair, and the woman can never know the spirit if she remains one with nature and unconsciousness. It is a paradox. She needs to be free from nature to gain consciousness, and at the same time her mission is to bring consciousness into union with nature. Thus forfeiting the freedom she has gained, she comes again under the power of Eros, but on a new level.

Eros was the male god who united with the feminine earth woman, and because of this union he became the feminine principle. It was not yet quite the woman's way, for she attempted to borrow the robes of Eros. As in life itself, one is not that thing of which one is merely assuming a role. She had yet to learn another way. Eros must not be cheated—in fact, cannot be cheated. Something has to be sacrificed, especially if that sacrifice is domination by Logos. Quite genuinely woman must reject that domination. Hence in the fantasy, the woman can no longer dwell unequal in the house of this most high god. It must, however, entail more than merely playing at being Eros, for that would not bring the co-operation of the god. The woman must come face to face with the wise old man from the standpoint of her real Eros or he will keep her imprisoned, for really he does not want to let her go. This surrendering of her hair, the domination of Logos and the animus, was the third great sacrifice.

But what of the old man himself as presented in the fantasy? As soon as the woman presents herself to him, he sees in her the Eve who is going to get him driven out of his paradise. She was more aware than he, for she had already been expelled, and here in his palace was yet another place that could tempt her with sleep. One finds in life that people who enter the spiritual world of ideas and even ideals are caught by them and, as far as the world is concerned, have fallen asleep. The woman had to be ever watchful, and when he calls her Eve she tells him he is not yet Adam. Adam means, literally, humankind. So this god is not yet human but still living the inhuman quality of the gods, aloof from the world, in a place where he was perfectly willing to keep her chained. But she had experienced and known her own inner change. We are often unaware of very great changes until we return to the old situation and find we are facing it with a new attitude or more consciousness. Going back into life after analysis is the time when one goes through the process of assimilation.

She had come to a place of patience and waiting, and, as often in analysis, things seem not to move. But here when the man moves, he moves farther away. He had not moved out of the castle and therefore had not been subjected to change, yet while he continued in this inert way nothing could really move, so he had to be shocked into action. It is just the same with the animus, who has to be shocked out of the castle in which he has lived. In life one is also up against a problem when it is a matter of the too sheltered life, and a woman's animus can live in the shelter of its leather-bound library of facts. When he is called upon to come into her household and live with her, become integrated as her real thinking rather than be an arbitrary opinion, he does not know how. She is the one who must lead him, show him her world and how things are, for it is as if he has never had knowledge of her feminine reality. If the lead is left to him he will carry her off again to library or castle. To live as a woman she has to get him to come with her into life, and to do this always means a sacrifice. In spite of the fact that the animus can destroy feminine life, a woman makes a terrific sacrifice to give up the power the animus can command. In fact she cannot really give it up, but knowledge of him helps her to use his power in a right way so that her feminine side has a chance also.

The old man had asked her not to try to find him—not on a new level. Man or the masculine principle wants unconscious woman. That is, if she remains unconscious she will be subject to and accept him unquestioningly. Yet it is when a woman gets to know the masculine otherness in herself that her real femininity has a chance to express itself. When Eros becomes a conscious principle the woman is capable of love. She can then see the outer man as he is, in his own right and not as her animus thinks he should be. Unconscious relationship can be of the most devouring nature. In the fantasy the woman's relationship with the painter was on the unconscious level which turned him into a devouring dragon from whom she had to escape and thus was forced into more consciousness.

The woman had demanded of the old man a sacrifice. It seems to be a secret attraction to God that he suffers with us. A god far off has not made the sacrifice to become human and experience human limitation. How can one who is bound by the earth love one far off who has never been bound? There is no common ground for understanding unless he comes down to earth, and he is the only one who can come down for he is the god. Therefore if God is to be known he has to be humanized; only then can the human race take steps toward the realm of God. Hence the importance of the human condition of the Son of God. The search is always to unite spirit and the material world, to fulfill again the first parents. The animus is the great archetype, the shaper of destinies and the link with God. He himself is truly a powerful god in the destiny of woman, as the anima is the powerful goddess of masculine psychology.

From the experience to which Wisdom had led the woman, from the sacrifice of her heart, her horse, her hair, she caught glimpses of a world beyond suffering and so had the strength to go further. In analysis each step may bring sacrifice and suffering, but also a surer knowledge that the unconscious does co-operate and also contains a wisdom in which we can trust. When we do not know, when there is seemingly no way, the wisdom of the unconscious can direct us. There dwell the wise old man and woman whom even more primitive tribes have learned to know and whom civilized man, in his grasping at the intellect, has lost.

Before the woman can bring about any change in the situation she must contact again the prostitute to get from her a feminine orientation to the problem. In analysis we come again and again to the same place, facing, as it were, the same problem, but the return is on a spiral where we know a little more even though the problem grows more difficult. Pride is always a difficult thing to surrender, and this is where the fourth sacrifice is demanded of her. She has arrived at a place of real ethical values, at a place where one can only step with true knowledge, devotion, and religious reverence. Pride and worldly values are really set aside. She sets her foot on the final path where pride cannot accompany her. This does not come early but at the end, because, having experienced so much, one becomes *the* sacrificer and is in danger of hubris. Hence it is pride which must finally bow before transpersonal demands. That is the toal sacrifice, to give up all, even the role of one who sacrifices. This is a conscious and mature act of sacrifice foregoing all claim, being willing to be utterly annihilated. So if by sacrifice one is willing to be personally given, then surely one has possessed oneself.[1]

The prostitute placed upon her finger a gold ring, the symbol of wholeness; such an action could give her strength, for quite naturally people are afraid when they approach the gods. While the divine old man is far off he is safe, but once he is actually in one's life he imposes a responsibility from which there is an inclination to shrink. The prostitute knows something of this when she gives her also the red robe, a garment worn by pagan gods and bearing the color of the Sun King. There seems to be a mingling of the pagan aspect with the Christian idea of "the bride." The ring she wore being the possession of the prostitute's mother points to wholeness within nature. Layard speaks of the ring or circle as "both the womb, the mother and the inviolate soul." [2] In making this gift she intuits a sacred non-personal motive in the journey the woman undertakes.

Back again at the castle, something is happening to the old man. He is angry at having to part with his beard, yet in spite of himself a change has set in. By his very interest and emotion he is being cornered by himself. His beard is demanded by the boy Eros, who can direct him and intends a union in which the man will have to attain to the human realm (or understanding) and realize he is not only a god above but one who is also on the level of his creation. The animus is a god with an inhuman aspect, so this represents also the humanizing of the animus. In the same way as the hair growing from the head represents thoughts, the beard can represent the spoken word. Words are the great achievement of the animus, and it is a rather humorous twist that he asks, on losing his beard, how he will know that he is wise. Women who have in the unconscious a bearded animus love words of wisdom, and words are often the aspect of Logos that holds woman spellbound and gains her devotion. Now this woman

[1] C. G. Jung, *Psychology and Religion: West and East*, page 257.
[2] John Layard, *Eranos XII. Incest Tabu and the Virgin Archetype*.

ignores the beard and sees beyond it, for she has a real contact with Wisdom herself and knows that the Great Mother's values lie not in words but in the experience life bestows.

The old man stripped of his beard is asked to approach the one who is part of nature. He, the spirit, in order to unite with the earth, must seek guidance from the earth woman. His aloofness must also be sacrificed if he is not to lose contact with his creation in the chthonic realm. This touches the problem of our day where the split is between Logos and Eros, between spirit and nature and the inner and outer reality.

That the woman went first, or took the leading role, is quite in accordance with ancient mysteries. The woman must make the first move, for she is the leader in the realm of Eros-relatedness. In life it is true that woman moving confidently in her own principle liberates man. This is not attained without certain sacrifices and a veneration for her Eros principle. In the mysteries, women made the sacrifice of virginity in the temples where the hieros gamos or sacred marriage was consummated by a priest. The act was an impersonal one and had nothing to do with the forms of secular marriage. Later this form of sacrifice was abolished and women went to the temple to sacrifice their hair, for all women went once to make a sacrifice to Eros before entering ordinary life.

In the fantasy the woman goes to the mountain, the self, as in the mysteries the temple was the self in whose precincts the sacred rites were performed. The man comes also to this sacred place. The hair had been sacrificed by the woman and the beard by the man, for this was a realm where words and worldly knowledge have no place in the mysteries of the soul, in the secrets of nature and the unio mystica.

It was to the mountain in both pagan and Christian times that people withdrew to commune with God. On the mountain and in the valleys, mists united heaven and earth; the self is a symbol draped about in mystery. The journey to the mountain is for the woman a labor of re-attainment, taken in order that she may realize who she is. She is one with nature and the Great Mother whose negative side is redeemed through love. It is this journey of love that brings fulfillment. This labor of love is an essential part of feminine psychology.

The journey to the mountain is in itself an archetypal motif.

Mount Meru of Indian philosophy is built up from things scattered about the world. Brought together they become the inner man where he can contemplate himself. Richard of St. Victor said, "It is the summit of knowledge to know that one knows oneself completely. The complete knowledge of a reasonable mind is a great high mountain. It is higher than peaks of all worldly knowledge; it looks down from above on all the wisdom of the world and on all knowledge of the world." There is the same idea in the Vulgate: "Learn to meditate, oh man, learn to meditate on thyself and thou wilt ascend in thine innermost. The more men improve daily in self-knowledge, the more they will climb over themselves. He who reaches the perfect knowledge has already reached the top of the mountain." [3] The historical significance of the mountain is also expressed in the idea of the Greek gods on Olympus, in Moses on Mount Sinai, and in Jesus's withdrawal to the mountain. The most meaningful mountain for the individual is that mountain built up from the four corners of his being, and in life many mountains have to be broken down that this transcendent one may stand alone.

So the mountain is the natural place to which the journey leads. It is a symbol for the Great Mother, and feminine mysteries have always been connected with the earth and matter. However transformed, they are essentially to do with the earth and the Great Mother or feminine principle.

In the fantasy we saw that when the woman needed guidance she was sent by the old man to find Wisdom. Her sacrifices and transformations must be in accordance with the feminine principle as prescribed by the Great Mother. It means for woman that neither man nor the animus can guide her behavior, for only according to her own principle can she truly develop as a feminine being. When woman meets man under his principle of Logos, it has to do with the spirit and its dominion to which she submits on a different level. Now when the old man was faced with moving into a relating role, he, too, consulted with Wisdom and the prostitute, which is quite in keeping with psychological facts. That is, in relationship man needs the Eros principle. Here he turns to the dictates of his heart in a place where Logos cannot guide him. For man it means recognition of the feminine principle, for woman it means sacrifice and acceptance.

[3] Vulgate. Psalm 63.

CHAPTER 8

The Myth continued via the Medium
of Clay Modeling
(The Jewel)

AT THIS stage of the Active Imagination, the model was produced which is pictured opposite. It portrays the mystical union. This conjunctio is the union of opposites, for woman with her spiritual self and for man with the soul. It is the union of sun and moon, conscious and unconscious, spirit and matter.

The heart the woman had carried and treasured was like the amulets used by the freeborn Roman children of the middle centuries. It distinguished them from the slaves. In the model the heart is now opened, revealing the new idea, the child who is a symbol of futurity.

This child is within the new center given her by Wisdom. It is the wisdom of the heart. The child is the new possibility, and the fact that it is an embryo within the heart points to the divine child and, as such, a special creation. The motif of the child will be dealt with more fully later. It is the precious small thing which has to be cared for tenderly in order that the divine experience may be safely born into the outer world.

From the model we see the old man not only parted with his beard but also with his clothing. Near and unclothed he is knowable and without shame. Adam and Eve clothed themselves to hide the consciousness of good and evil, and here the clothes naturally fall away as the opposites are overcome. In analysis one has to drop the clothing of the persona to face oneself, for

Plotinus I.6:
"To attain to Good we must ascend to the highest state, and fixing our
gaze thereon, lay aside the garments we donned when descending here
below; just as in the Mysteries, those who are permitted to penetrate into
the inner recesses of the sanctuary, after having purified themselves, lay
aside every garment, and advance stark naked."

while one feels shame one can never face oneself. There is no room in the journey to the self for the ego trappings that clothes can represent.

"His disciples said unto him: When will thou be manifest to us and when shall we see thee? He said: When ye shall be naked and not ashamed." [1]

Renewed he shook his aged mantles off
Into the fires—Then glorious bright, exalting in his joy
He sounding rose into the heavens in naked majesty,
In radiant Youth.[2]

The change had a rejuvenating effect on the old man. Every direct contact with the Divine Old Man rejuvenates his life in the world. A dove appeared in the last three models. It is the dove of Aphrodite, of Sophia, and is an attribute of the Great Mother which leads to love. In the two models that follow no dove appears, for its work is done. It is transformed and instead there comes the Tree of Life and then Mary.

In *Aion*, Jung quotes from Plotinus, a mystic of the third century, as follows: "Self-knowledge reveals the fact that the soul's natural movement is not in a straight line, unless indeed it has undergone some deviation. On the contrary it circles around something interior around a circle. Now the center is that from which proceeds the circle, that is, around the principle from which she proceeds: and tending toward it, she will attach herself to it, as indeed all souls should do. The souls of the divinities ever direct themselves toward it, and that is the secret of their divinity; for divinity consists in being attached to the center. . . . Anyone who withdraws from it is a man who has remained un-unified, or who is a brute." Jung continues by saying: "Here the point is the center of a circle that is created, so to speak, by the circumambulation of the soul. But this point is the center of all things, a God-image. This is the idea that still underlies the mandala symbols in modern dreams." [3]

In this fantasy creation came from the center, the old man who,

[1] Dunkerley: I believe this to be from uncanonical writings (Oxyrhyncus).
[2] William Blake.
[3] Page 218.

sitting in the center of the lake which had flowed from him, was also a God-image. The whole activity is to return to this center. The origin is the goal.

In a woman's case the emphasis is on the activity of the soul and points to a very special demand of her Eros nature. She has to seek out the god and bring him into her world. In life if woman allows the animus to remain a remote ruler of her destiny, an un-unified autonomy, he is indeed the brute referred to by Plotinus, in just the same way as the man whose soul has never drawn him to the center is in the same category.

The ideas inherent in the model and the love song could only be expressed symbolically. They reveal the archetype of the mystical union which is a wordless experience, but which is the powerful force within all relationship between man and woman. It touches the cosmic myth, the union of heaven and earth which underlies all creative processes.

Sophia or Wisdom was the earth reunited with the god in the sacred marriage. Mary too was the earth from which Christ was born. "Because the earth, as creative aspect of the feminine, rules over vegetative life, it holds the secret of the deeper and original form of 'conception and generation' upon which all animal life is based. For this reason the highest and most essential Mysteries of the Feminine are symbolized by the earth and its trans-formation." [4]

In the fantasy the man leaves her, for such is the case in all inner experience. It is not the image which remains, for the image has conferred the experience, and it is the experience alone which is durable. This is what is both lasting and efficacious. Now this of course is the very place where the last and final sacrifice has to be made. She has been led to the profound experience which gives itself up and asks for nothing in return. It is a sacrifice on the altar of Ishtar, where one enters a mystery which can never be seen. This is the fifth sacrifice. It is the quinta essentia, which draws all the other sacrifices within itself. Here it is a matter of facing that which is transcendent where there is no ego left at all, where all is surrendered on the altar of God. This is the experience that formulates outer life. Where love is given for its sake alone and where the ego makes no demands, —

[4] Erich Neumann, *The Great Mother,* page 51.

life takes on a deeper meaning. Often with such inner realization love will come into a woman's life from outside.

The man had to withdraw to become her reality, for to remain he still would have been "the other." Withdrawal really meant he was united with her. That from which she had been born was the center of her being. Christ's ascent meant that his spirit lived with his disciples and must not be left in Him alone. But of Wisdom, Neumann has said: "Sophia does not vanish in the nirvana-like abstraction of a masculine spirit: like the scent of blossoms her spirit always remains attached to the earthly foundations of reality." [5] The woman had to come again to the world alone. Jung says: "Higher consciousness or knowledge going beyond what we are conscious of at the moment is the equivalent of being all alone in the world. The loneliness expresses the conflict between the bearer or symbol of higher consciousness and his surroundings." [6] It is as if the myth portrays the loneliness which follows the inner realization when one has gone beyond one's surroundings, a fact which can never be really conveyed to another. However, the fact that Sophia remains adds something of spiritual importance to banal reality. It is in the myth as if Wisdom insists the woman come back to this reality, to realize her sacrifice and know herself as part of nature. In fact it seems that the self, knowing the heights to which one can be lifted by contact with the living spirit, insists that she remain humble and not fall into inflation and longing for the spirit. Sophia has been in the picture from the beginning, ready to allot tasks, sometimes appearing as a power for good and sometimes as a power for evil, in order that things will work toward return to the center on a higher level. This same Wisdom remains to comfort her in her hour of sacrifice, no human type of comfort, but a demand of the self for the fulfillment of allotted tasks.

The divine union, unio mystica, breaks the incest taboo on the level of spiritual union with God and transcends human prohibition. It is the union with one's self, with one's own being, and the overcoming of one's own division. In a woman's psychology the process of individuation is always connected with the

[5] Ibid., page 325.

[6] C. G. Jung and C. Kerenyi, *Introduction to a the Science of Mythology*, page 122.

problem of love. It includes not only the love of another, but the love of oneself, which means to accept oneself in a way that counts, to allow oneself the right to wholeness. This union can never be attempted cheaply or one would pay a deadly price. In the fantasy the idea leads quite naturally to the place of union. There could be no other way. It expresses a psychic process in mankind which is cradled deeply in the unconscious. It demands the highest development of the sexual instinct, or as Layard says: "transformed sexual instincts in terms of the union of the soul with God. . . . The state of oneness with the mother while yet within the womb, typified by Adam and Eve in Eden, is the epitome of the incestuous union in which all life begins, and also to which it must return, though on a higher plane." [7] Between the first state and the second lies the possibility of individuation—the lonely path leading to the "Soul's brideship with God." The search culminates with the union with the self, the discovering of the lapis, the jewel and the treasure of the heart. It cannot be understood rationally, and only through experience does one begin to know.

I believe such an experience comes mostly in the second half of life. Union on the physical plane expresses the ultimate union and needs to be lived, and only later one begins to search for the union with the self. It is the process of individuation which releases energy from solely biological goals and transforms it, placing it at the service of the psyche; a transformation which affects the whole character of the individual and alters the direction of life. The "I-ness" has a new center and a new meaning. The shift of meaning also enhances old things in the old place, for the "I" desires lose their pettiness when faced with the non-personal. Here one finds the instinct of true culture, reflection, and meaning. A medical friend said to me recently that he experienced advancing years as being the slowing of the step a little, as being a little more tired from the physical exertion, but that it carried a great compensation, and most satisfactory, in the growing activity of the reflecting mind and the spirit, and the new energies which widened the horizon. People discover that and wonder as they find increasing satisfaction in the new field. Usually they

[7] John Layard, *Eranos XII. Incest Tabu and the Virgin Archetype*, page 259.

are people who have lived life, and individuation is a process of living and becoming more conscious out of the experience. Life is more than eating, sleeping, and pleasure. The man who really lives accepts his task, great or small, *knows* that he is living and knows that he suffers, and can let life unfold. Then his energies widen his horizon. Perhaps nature has a great wisdom in slowing the step a little. It is a far cry from inertia. It may be the slowing up which precedes creation, creation on a level which is forever evolving, for surely man has not reached his culmination. Those declining years, when the world is no longer the great challenge, when one's work is done, offer the time of the inner challenge placed upon man, "never to sell the jewel." The birth of the divine child is a symbol of this inner growth, and the importance of the child motif is its futurity. What is the future of the closing years of life? Surely this can only be answered on the spiritual plane.

The union with God expressed in the language of love is common among mystics and in the Song of Songs expresses a mystical experience. To maintain one's conscious rational standpoint after such an experience means holding the two together. Not to be caught by the experience and not to let it sink again and disappear in the unconscious means to stand between and reconcile them. Only where sex is repressed and correspondingly overvalued can we speak of compensation in a religious experience. Sexual symbolism was used of old to express union with and love for God, because it is the nearest most understood symbolical expression of giving oneself to another. Actually sexuality in itself is a sort of myth where the universal drama enters the microcosm. Philip of Alexandria regarded the Sacred Marriage as the chief of all the mysteries. He says: "For the congress of men for the procreation of children makes virgins women. But when God begins to associate with the soul, He brings it to pass that she who was formerly woman becomes virgin again. . . . the oracle hath been careful to say that God is the husband not of the virgin—for a virgin is subject to change and death—but of virginity." [8] Esther Harding says: "When she has passed through an experience analogous to the ancient prostitution in the temple, the elements of desirousness and possessiveness have been given

[8] G. R. S. Mead, *Thrice Greatest Hermes.*

up, transmuted through the appreciation that her sexuality, her instinct are expressions of divine life force whose experience is of inestimable value, quite apart from their fulfillment on the human scale. It is impossible to explain the transformation that takes place when instinctive love is accepted in this way and assimilated, for it is one of those mysteries and inexplicable changes that belong in the realm of the psychological, the realm where spiritual and physical meet. The transformation from the physical to the spiritual is indeed a never-ending mystery which is beyond our human understanding. It is, however, a matter of actual observation that through an experience of this kind love emerges which sees the situation of the other person and can unselfishly sympathize and understand." [9]

[9] *Woman's Mysteries*, page 153.

CHAPTER 9

Concluding Movements of the Fantasy
with Comments
(The Realization)

FROM HERE on the fantasy, as far as we will continue it, was represented in clay. On the opposite page is an illustration of a woman standing within the circle of water which flows from a fountain. The whole picture gives one the feeling of acceptance. She is again within the waters from whence she came. When life has run its course one comes again to the sea or the lake, as the

---

From *Signs* by Rudolf Koch
In regard to the cross within the circle as seen on the model the author makes these remarks:

    — Represents salt as an old chemical sign.
    | Represents saltpeter or niter, which is a fertilizer.
    — = passive female element.
    | = active male element.
    ⊕ = male element pervading female and so creation takes place.
        Used as a sign for the elements it is the earth.
        It is also a sign for Mary and for Wotan.

Inventing runes, Odin said,
"I know that I hung   On that tree
On a wind-rocked tree   Of which no one knows
Nine whole nights,   From what root it springs."
With spear wounded,   Odin's Rune Song (Thorpe)
And to Odin offered   from *Myth of Norsemen*
Myself to myself;   (Guerber).

⊕ is also the mathematical symbol of the Name of Names, I H V H, the unutterable name. Teth.

river flowed to the sea, the great sea, in the beginning of the
fantasy. The fountain means constancy; it is the eternal flow of
life. There is a natural tendency to return which leads not back
to childhood but to childlikeness. The acceptance is the love of
fate which must end in human death and the surrendering of
the individual to the principle of life. The tree is life itself, and
standing thus she is extended upon the tree, yet she is within
the circle, for the very consciousness she now has is as a circle
around her. Nicholas of Cusa saw the circular sea, which
replenishes itself from a spring, as an allegory of God.[1] In ancient
writings Wisdom herself is compared with the tree. She is the
cedar and the palm, etc. A tree always stood upon the altars of the
Mother Goddess.[2]

The following is the Soliloquy which followed the contemplation of the model.

> How great the message whispered in my heart
> The source of Life, the source of every art
> Surrounds me as the fountain waters flow.
> And as the tree they lead to earth and sky.
> Alone I was and yet alone because
> One journeys singly in the realm of God.
> So silent! 'Tis silently revealed
> My father in me dwells and I in Him
> We need each other as the earth the sun.
> In timeless moment too I see
> The "now" of immortality.
> Those aeons past the future knew
> Stretched out by time as ever new.
> The heart grasps things it cannot yet express
> And lisping words convey them even less.
> Yet hands can mold a form which seems to say
> "Life here I stand, there is no other way."

It would seem that such an attitude would bring the animus
into a role of real creativity and sharing. That which comes from

[1] C. G. Jung, *Aion*, page 216.
[2] See Song of Solomon 4, 8.

the heart belongs to Eros, and there one sacrifices illusions and devotes oneself to reality. Longing for the spiritual life can lead one out of reality, and the union of spirit and nature brings one again into the earth and actual life. One has to pass through the rituals of a mystery cult and for woman, as in Eleusis, it means something grows in the earth.

The place where one discovers "I and the Father are one" is just the place where one has to step down. Herein lies the great danger, for the idea is numinous and possessing. Even though one has known such things as metaphysical facts all one's life, they burst upon one afresh out of such dynamic experience. A self is realized which is not ego as such. Between the ego and the unconscious is born a wider personality, and this leads into the collective, for one's own uniqueness is that particular way in which collective things have come together.

A quality of the self is timelessness, an always-has-been-ness. And it always has been. The self includes the opposites and among them the past and the future. It touches the archetype of eternity. "I and my Father are one" transcends literal truth, and yet it is the great truth. In an ego sense it would be a blasphemy diminishing God, but in a psychological sense it touches on the divine immanence. It speaks as in the Soliloquy of the eternal image which patterns phenomena. With the insight such experience bestows, one comes again into the phenomenal world of ordinary reality to add to it greater dimension and understanding.

In the Tibetan Book of the Great Liberation, Evans-Wentz speaks of the Great Liberation as the *knowing* that Sangsara and Nirvana are eternally and indistinguishably one, and Plotinus says it is necessary for the many "to amalgamate himself with the Principle which he possesseth innately." According to Tibetan Buddhism, otherness and self are identical, and when man wars against this otherness he wars against his own body, his own oneness in the self.

To be in the "now" one is not caught by the past or extended into the future, but is more fully in life, more acutely aware. The "now of immortality" brings things into the present, into Tao. It is as if the long trail of personal and non-personal past and the hopes and intuition of the future are suddenly close

together, enfolded in the "now." This coming together means also a preparation for death. The knowledge one has gained is not knowledge of the ego (which is often thought of as self-knowledge) but knowledge of the self.

The self for woman is feminine, and though the self cannot be equated with the image of God, there is a secret connection. Perhaps it is now clear why I have stressed that the woman is a self figure and not the ego. She is completed by the other feminine beings and her union with the god. Individuation is life in God. This myth of the unconscious shows symbolically the process which leads to this union. The self symbolizes the totality. The ego is not the self, but the progress of ego toward selfhood is made clear.

For a woman to discover the feminine self is of great importance, for in the masculine trinity there has been no place where she has fitted. Mary is an archetype who brings woman again into the divine hierarchy, as shown by the Assumption accorded her in the Catholic Church. Therefore it is not unexpected, though not consciously done, that the next model brought forth the figure of the Madonna. The Great Mother approaches and blesses. She is part of the quaternity, adding to the masculine trinity. The archetype of the feminine in woman's psychology forms another trinity completed by the masculine fourth, that is, spirit or Logos. In this case the feminine trinity stands opposite the masculine trinity. Sophia is the feminine spirit, the breath of God, the one who said: "I came out of the mouth of the most High." She is the one who describes herself as Logos,[3] and so in the feminine trinity is the Holy Ghost. She is the real and moving livingness of the created world, closely one with God in the perpetual hieros gamos.[4]

[3] Proverbs 8.

[4] In *Psychology and Alchemy* (pages 144-45) Jung speaks of Sophia as the anima "the dark and dreaded maternal womb." He says: "The female element in the deity is kept very dark. The interpretation of Sophia as the Holy Ghost being considered heretical. . . . He was the mediator of birth in the flesh, who enabled the deity to shine forth in the darkness of the world. No doubt it was this association which caused the Holy Ghost to be suspected of femininity, for Mary was the dark earth of the field." In the fantasy Wisdom's work brings the woman into mundane reality. Wisdom's work was

In the final model there appears Mary, the woman and the child. Mary protected and cared for Jesus and is a symbol of individuation for woman as Jesus is for man. Quite naturally the Madonna replaces the tree. She is the tree of life which blossomed and bore fruit. She is the wellspring and the fountain. The previous model was one of passivity, a turning to the center, and a realization. Thus there follows a creation; a new birth; a new beginning.

As Our Lady of Wisdom, Mary is represented in Church symbolism reading the seventh chapter of the Wisdom of Solomon, opened at the words . . . "For she is the breath of the power of God and a pure influence flowing from the Glory of the Almighty." [5] Of the beloved of Solomon it is said: "A garden enclosed is my sister, my spouse; a spring shut up, a fountain sealed. . . . A fountain of gardens, a well of living waters and streams from Lebanon." [6] Bayley informs us that "the uncanonical Gospel according to the Hebrews relates that after the baptism of Christ 'the entire fountain of the Holy Spirit descended and rested upon Him'; and this symbolic fountain is evidently a synonym for the Dove of the Holy Spirit of the canonical Gospels." [7] This now explains the absence of the Dove, which appeared in earlier models connected with the fantasy, and disappeared when the "fountain" and "Mary" became evident in a new form.

The fantasy has contained many references to water, the sea, the streams, the mists, and the fountain. In myths and fairy tales, water, in whatever form, has the connotation of the cleansing and refreshing qualities of the spirit. Sophia lingered upon the waters of the "beginning"; she is, as Mary after her, the

the incarnating process. It would seem that Wisdom, the third person of the feminine trinity, becomes the fifth, the quinta essentia of an equal quaternity. (See footnote 8, page 119.) Sophia is also the perpetual movement, the serpent moving through the twelve signs of the Zodiac in the Persian illustration of Boundless Time and Aion. This brings Eternal Wisdom into the concept of time where she is more available to man.

[5] Mrs. H. Jenner, Our Lady in Art, page 15.
[6] Song of Solomon 4:12-15.
[7] Harold Bayley, Lost Language of Symbolism, page 240.

fountain of life; the dewdrop in which is embodied the whole world. "Therefore God give thee of the dew of heaven." [8]

It was the virgin who by acceptance and willingness to the spirit brought about the incarnation of God which linked heaven and earth. She is an archetype akin to Wisdom—Sophia and mother goddesses. She is called the Myrrh of the Sea. As Sophia, she is the womb from which the worlds were begotten and born, and separated through creation, the world from the spirit; as Mary she is the infinite in finite form who brings about the union of heaven and earth, and who, as Bride of Heaven, is co-redeemer with God. She becomes again the beginning.[9]

For the writer of the myth it symbolized a beginning, the beginning of life understood as purposive and leading beyond itself. So the actual myth ends as far as this work is concerned with it, a fantasy which commences with the beginning of mankind and leads into futurity and life beyond death. When people lead the traditional life, they never break with accepted things but are one with them, they are less likely to receive these messages from the unconscious. If they have broken away from the old ways and accepted forms, something has to be found to replace them. One has a chance to know who one is. It seems necessary for a woman to know she is woman and differentiate between herself and the spiritual animus, that she may consciously unite with him where on this level he becomes the enhancement of her mind.[10]

[8] Genesis 27:28.
Bayley says in *Lost Language of Symbolism*, Vol. 1, page 167, "Wisdom meant more than truth. It was later to personify the Celestial Influence which at a later period was described as the 'Holy Spirit.'" The Virgin Mary is our Lady of Wisdom.

[9] She gave birth to the God-man who hung upon the cross, who can only be redeemed from the cross by rebirth within the individual.

[10] While it has been pointed out that Eros is relatedness and also the feminine realm and Logos is discrimination and the masculine realm, it does not mean that woman lives or should live Eros and man Logos. These two are a syzygy within both man and woman. Logos and Eros, that is, conscious discrimination and diffused awareness, are a way of consciousness in their own right, and inherent in mankind. When man uses Logos it regards only the thing itself, and when Eros enters into the picture he realizes the effects and the ramifications of the thing itself. When a woman uses Eros consciousness

So while we have taken one section, in itself complete, the fantasy continues further.

The final model reveals the child which was seen in the heart in an earlier model. The child has a special significance which I think could best be presented by extracts from Jung in *Science of Mythology*. He says: "One of the essential features of the child-motif is its futurity. The child is potential future. Hence the occurrence of the child-motif in the psychology of the individual signifies as a rule an anticipation of future developments, even though at first sight it may seem to be a retrospective configuration. Life is a flux, a flowing into the future, and not a stoppage or a backwash. It is therefore not surprising that so many of the mythological saviors are child-gods. This corresponds exactly to our experience in the psychology of the individual, which shows that the 'child' paves the way for a future change of personality. In the individuation process, it anticipates the figure that comes from the synthesis of conscious and unconscious elements in the personality. It is therefore a *uniting symbol* which unites the opposites; a mediator, bringer of healing, that is, *one who makes whole*. Because it has this meaning, the child-motif is capable of the numerous transformations mentioned above. It can be expressed by roundness, the circle or sphere, or else by the quaternity as another form of wholeness. I have called this consciousness-transcending wholeness the 'self.' " [11] "The 'child' is born out of the womb of the unconscious, begotten out of the depths of human nature, or rather out of living Nature herself. It is a personification of vital forces quite outside the limited range of our conscious mind; of possible ways and means of which our one-sided conscious mind knows nothing; a wholeness which embraces the very depths of Nature. It represents the strongest, the most ineluctable urge in every being, namely the urge to realize itself. It is, as it were, an incarnation of the *inability to do otherwise, equipped with all the powers of nature and instinct,*

---

she thinks in a feeling tone, is given to sympathetic understanding, but when she adds Logos consciousness, she discriminates as to the right, the wrong, the justification, etc., of the sympathy. It is a knowledge of these distinct ways of consciousness which molds them into a syzygy and lessens the possibility of animus or anima possession.

[11] C. G. Jung and C. Kerenyi, *Introduction to a Science of Mythology*, page 115.

whereas the conscious mind is always getting tied up in its supposed ability to do otherwise. The urge and compulsion to self-realization are *a law of nature* and thus of invincible power, even though its effect at the start is insignificant and improbable." [12] "The symbols of the self arise in the depths of the body and they express its materiality every bit as much as the structure of the perceiving consciousness expresses it. The symbol is thus a living body, corpus et anima. . . ." [13]

In analysis, the child means bringing what one has learned into the here and now and leads to the all important thing, one's attitude to life. Knowing who one is creates an attitude in which one is not lost but lives more consciously, allowing the growth of the divine child. The new attitude is related to the self. Active Imagination brings symbols which point again to life. When the veils of the unconscious are withdrawn we see the myth and the alchemical process. It reveals the way of rebirth which involves suffering as if one goes through the experience of classical antiquity. It is a revelation of the secrets of ancient mystery cults and of Christianity. It shows again the religious attitude which is still alive in the unconscious today and which speaks of that which is always a divince mystery. Free spirit is united with static nature. To experience for oneself divine, ineffable, inexpressible facts, which cannot be intellectualized, plants one on surer ground and gives meaning to life. It is a rebirth in which the Divine Child has a chance to grow and become an inner responsibility which heightens and deepens human experience. The "Old Man" disappears and is renewed in the "Child."

Through such experiences lost values are restored. The feminine takes its place in the redemption of the human being from halfness to wholeness. One enters, as it were, the temple of the goddess as the ancients did in order to experience oneself completely. In analysis one brings to this altar one's instincts, emotions, and one's smallest self. In the psyche is the living mystery and in the temple the veil is lifted that one might perceive it. The lifting of this veil of Maya is an experience of death and rebirth.

[12] Ibid., page 123.
[13] Ibid., page 127.

The writer of the fantasy was unconsciously concerned with the non-ego, so it is impersonal and not personal psychology which is revealed. While the process brings to light unconscious processes within the person, she herself is not *the* unconscious. The unconscious advances toward her that it may be transformed through her conscious attention and attitude. This is the sacred task of those who take the "Night Sea Journey." The work is being done in them and through them as if they had been chosen for the sacred trust which means the transformation of the collective unconscious into something human. This power is not in man even though he is selected, but transcends him even in his highest moments. As Jung says in *Visions*, "It begins at the bottom, as it were, as if the whole world had to be built anew, or as if nothing had ever happened before, and then it carries the thought through until it reaches the stage that is not yet and never has been; it reaches the future. It is often as if the series covered the whole way, as if each series extended from hell to heaven, from the beginning to the end, as if it were a complete cycle more or less clearly formulated. All who have gone through such stretches of the inner desert or the inner wilderness have the feeling they have thereby lost their former world. The movement forward naturally leads you into the world, because the world is the only place where you can create. You cannot create when you are withdrawn into the air entirely; you need the world because it is the raw material. . . . But the withdrawal from the world is only useful when the spirit must be demonstrated. These things do not come out of the life we know. It is because that is exhausted we turn in, and here in the unexpected place, new life begins to flow again." [14] Touching such archetypal figures, who are themselves non-personal, has a tremendous effect on the individual.

We noticed in the fantasy that the feminine figures Wisdom, the prostitute, and the woman form a trinity. There is a triad in feminine psychology which is completed by the masculine fourth for wholeness. This triad is the mystery of mother and daughter and the feminine spirit. In the Eleusinian Mysteries the maiden was, as Kerenyi says, "a primal being born of a primal element. . . . Her virginity and the virginity of all Kores in the world of

[14] C. G. Jung, *Visions* 3.

the Greek gods is not anthropomorphic but a quality of the un-
adulterated primal element which had given her birth." [15] The
triadic idea preceded and was more naïve than the later concept
of the trinity.

The fantasy also shows a triad of the masculine in the old man,
the painter, and the dealer, both of the latter being different
aspects of the old man himself. Figures appear to melt into each
other in Active Imagination as they do in myths, and it seems
as if the unconscious asks not to be classified too sharply so that
the many aspects may be revealed. The woman is helped to deal
with the man in his triple aspect . . . to bring him to a unity.
She suffered the darkness in order to learn. It was the devil in
Faust who said he intended evil and achieved good. It would
seem that the feminine forces, for all their darkness within the
framework of Eros, work against the destructive aspect of the
spirit. Woman belongs as the Kore to past and future. She is her
mother and her daughter, extending up and down, backward and
forward in a peculiar oneness which gives a feeling of immortality.
It is the feminine world which opposes the violation of its basic
feminine principle. An attempt was made to steal away the heart
of Eros, a procedure which brought up all the energies of the
feminine trinity.

The three feminine beings in mythology are a lower triad
which has to do with nature and the earth, and opposite them
is the upper or masculine triad which has to do with the spirit.
This unified triad completes a quaternity where spirit is united
with the earth.[16] "The original man Nous stepped down from the

---

[15] Jung and Kerenyi, op. cit., page 208.

[16] Actually it is not triadic. The triad is made up of equal beings. The
Trinity or tri-unity is three which are one. So I see this particular work as
more trinitarian. As I mentioned earlier the triad is more naïve, while the
trinitarian concept is the result of the act of reflection. In ancient times the
trinity was Father, Mother, and Son. As it was given more and more consideration in the realm of the Logos, the feminine idea was dropped out
completely and the Holy Ghost became masculine. Now the Holy Ghost is
the fertilizer, he fertilized Mary but his connection with Sophia was naïvely
or indiscriminately revealed by the fact that he was the Dove. (Note: The
Dove appeared in all models up to the final sacrifice.) The spirit descended
as a dove to Mary and also to Jesus at Bethany. The dove had always been
the bird of both Aphrodite and Sophia. The dove came to represent the

heavens to earth to become wrapped in the embrace of physis—a primordial image running right through alchemy." [17] The mystical union takes place in the realm of the feminine. Through her the mystery comes into the world to be seen on earth. God is an archetypal image in the soul of man; he appeared to the ancients as an anthropomorphic god, and it would seem there lives in the inner world of man a need to make again this anthropomorphic god in order to relate to him. As the woman says, how can one know that which is far off? A question which is followed in metaphysical speculation by the question of the divine nature in mankind, and the created world.

---

spirit. According to how the spirit functions, it seems to be at times more of Sophia and at others more of the Holy Ghost. Sophia is love and the Holy Ghost is understanding and is the intellectual function. When love and understanding are balanced they are one. The meeting of the spirit and the earth is the union of Sophia and the Holy Ghost and thus they are transcendent in the union of the masculine and feminine trinities. This is the equal quaternity with them as the transcendent fifth. We could say then the old man also is the Holy Ghost, who fertilizes the feminine and disappears. As the Divine pair, they, Wisdom and the old man, are one.

[17] C. G. Jung, *Practice of Psychotherapy*, page 245.

CHAPTER **10**

Some General Indications of the Fantasy

A FEW general remarks on the whole fantasy.

That life should come from the water or tears, as we found depicted in the fantasy, is not only a motif of mythology but also a scientifically recognized fact. Hence it is not merely a mythological idea. Kerenyi says in *Science of Mythology* that: "It is not a groundless generalization to say that mythology tells of the origins or at least of what originally was. When it tells of a younger generation of gods of Greek history, these too signify the beginning of the world . . . the world the Greeks lived in under the rule of Zeus. The gods are so original that a new world is always born with a new god . . . a new epoch or new aspect of the world. . . . Though they are all present all the time, the mythologems which unfold in narrative form what is contained in the figures of the gods are always set in a primordial time. This return to primordiality is a basic feature of every mythology.

"Mythology provides a foundation in so far as the teller of myths, by living out his story, finds his way back to primitive times. Suddenly, without any digression or searching on his part, without any studious investigation or effort, he finds himself in the primordiality that is his concern, in the midst of the beginning of which he is speaking. (What are the *beginnings* in whose midst a man can really find himself?) To which of them can he dive down straightaway? The *beginnings* are as numerous as the elements composing man's world, including man himself. He has his own *beginning*, the *beginning* of his organic being from which he continually creates himself. He experiences his own origin as a developed organism, thanks to a kind of identity, as though he were a reverberation of it multiplied a thousandfold and his origin were the first note struck. He experiences it as his own absolute *beginning*, a beginning since when he was a unity fusing in itself all the contradictions of his nature and life to be. To this origin, understood as the beginning of a new world-unit, the mythologem of the divine child points. The mythologem of the maiden goddess points to yet another *beginning*, also experienced as one's own origin but which is at the same time the *beginning* of countless beings before and after oneself, and by virtue of which the individual is endowed with infinity already in the germ. . . . Going back into ourselves in this way and rendering an account of it, we experience and proclaim the very foundation of our being; that is to say, we are grounding ourselves." [1]

The sad and lonely old man in the fantasy is the distant unknown God who fails to be recognized in the rushtime of modern living. He is the lonely God, the root and the beginning who awaits recognition. In the end the sad God becomes the triumphal God, who is now a living reality in the new consciousness. [2]

We do not know the archetypes. We contact the archetypal image which gives us a nod and a hint of how things are and always have been and of what lies behind the image. In getting back to the beginning we in some way get a comprehension of it all. Generally speaking, life is taken for granted because

[1] C. G. Jung and C. Kerenyi, *Introduction to a Science of Mythology*, page 11. In this quotation I have translated the Greek into *beginning* and *beginnings*, which might not be exactly Kerenyi's meaning.

[2] N.B. Another reference to the old man could be made. He, as Proteus-Oannes the "Old Man of the Sea" was the great wisdom and the great teacher who is difficult to grasp and hold. Homer indicates the difficulty in grasping and holding wisdom in the story of Menelaus. When Menelaus, husband of Helen, was stranded, a sea-maiden daughter of the old man came to show him how to find the old man of the sea, and how to hold on to him, for he would change into many forms including fire and water, but if his capturers clung firmly he would eventually assume his original form and give needed information and advice. When such a figure appears in Active Imagination it suggests a knowledge which reaches beyond, and at the same time suggests it must be grasped firmly and sought after. What ultimately comes from it is according to the capacity and sincerity of the doer or the dreamer, if such archetypal figures appear in dreams.

things have "been" for so long and we merely accept the way things go. We do not realize that the archetype is attempting to draw closer to our human life. One cannot go beyond the phenomenal aspect. No matter what statements we make, nothing is explained about primordiality or the beginnings. What is proved is that man's soul searches back to its beginning. "The archetype," say Jung, "is a psychic organ present in all of us." It is important not to equate the image with the transcendental, the unknowable, about which it speaks and to which it points. The image which speaks of God is not God. The image brings us knowledge by using a form through which we are gripped by its higher meaning. The symbol or the image stretches up and down at the same time, and so it speaks of heaven and earth; that which transcends us is spoken of in terms of that in which we live, so that in us they are united. The unspeakable is dimly spoken through our usable coin.

The general idea before Darwin was that specific species did exist which were held to be permanent and immutable though some variation in form was also admitted. Each was accepted as a special creation. The impact of Darwinism turned general thought to watch more specifically the idea of man's growth out of lower animal and vegetable form to what it is today. The story of Genesis had grown into a myth rather than an account of creation, and so it took deeper insight to connect scientific discoveries with man's religious belief. Here Jung's work is of paramount importance, holding as it does the hand of both science and religion. Many scientists looked upon life as an ethical code relative to a particular species, as a materialized process of ethics. On one hand the idea of egotism and on the other that of altruism as being the great factor in man's growth. Yet each is embedded in the foundations of life. No more can we know of ultimate things than we can solve the riddle of the beginnings. The myth in man gives us a glimpse, for it comes from that which has been lived since man became conscious, and it is man himself who is weaving the silver thread of eternal things.

"Myths," says Jung in *Science of Mythology*, "are original revelations of the preconscious psyche, involuntary statements about unconscious psychic happenings, and anything but allegories of physical processes. Such allegories would be an idle amusement for an unscientific intellect. Myths, on the contrary, have a vital meaning. Not merely do they represent, they *are* the mental life of the primitive tribe, which immediately falls to pieces and decays when it loses its mythological heritage, like a man who has lost his soul. A tribe's mythology is its living religion, whose loss is always and everywhere, even among the civilized, a moral catastrophe. But religion is a vital link with psychic processes independent of and beyond consciousness, in the dark hinterland of the psyche. Many of these unconscious processes may be indirectly occasioned by consciousness, but never by conscious choice. Others appear to arise spontaneously, that is to say, from no discernible or demonstrable conscious cause." [3]

"Modern psychology treats the products of unconscious imagination as self-portraits of what is going on in the unconscious, or as statements of the unconscious psyche about itself. They fall into two categories. Firstly, fantasies (including dreams) of a personal character, which go back unquestionably to personal experiences; things forgotten or repressed, and thus can be completely explained by individual anamnesis. Secondly, fantasies (including dreams) of an impersonal character, which cannot be reduced to experiences in the individual's past, and thus cannot be explained as something individually acquired. These fantasy-pictures undoubtedly have their closest analogues in mythological types. We must therefore assume that they correspond to certain collective (and not personal) structural elements of the human psyche in general, and, like the morphological elements of the human body, are inherited. . . ." [4] "Archetypes were, and still are, psychic forces that demand to be taken seriously, and they have a strange way of making sure of their effect. Always they were the bringers of protection and salvation, and their violation has as its consequence the "perils of the soul," known to us from the psychology of primitives. Moreover, they are the infallible causes of neurotic and even psychotic disorders, behaving exactly like neglected or maltreated physical organs or organic functional systems." [5]

[3] Jung and Kerenyi, op. cit., pages 101ff.
[4] Ibid., page 102.
[5] Ibid., page 105.

A myth is a spontaneous fantasy that does not try to explain anything, belonging as it does to the collective unconscious. It is more the revelation of how things are than any explanation of them, and a modern myth or fantasy portrays just these things which have been portrayed throughout the ages. Because it is free from overwhelming conscious intervention, it can contain doctrinal truths which transcend limitations and illusions by which man is fettered and point the way the unconscious is attempting psychic health. A psychology that ignores the collective unconscious ignores the very roots from which health springs. If a conscious, generally accepted validity is attempted, paradoxes of the psyche are sent underground and a normality attempted which is sterile. When the collective unconscious is given credit, the source of consciousness is tapped in darkest and most bewildering places which include also the healing.

Mythology does not state a truth per se but acts as a sort of non-deliberate divination. It acts in a magical way, transcending the limitations of consciously adapted life. It disregards the impossible, for it is beyond ego and does not refer to what "I am" as such, but to what is for all time. That it is timeless, beyond time, is something indicated by the age of the old man. Touching that freedom, it touches what one is in a wider sense. The myth being numinous nods its head at the observer, but it cannot be interpreted to mean this or that specifically. And should we try to fit it into the facts rather than follow its story, we lose it. The myth is not concerned with facts as man knows them; it speaks out of the unknown with all its magic art, ignoring the deadly sterility of man's conception of reality. When we try to fit the unknowable god into a prejudice, we lose this numinosity and religion becomes an intellectual concern. Knowledge always includes the unknowable, even as science is based on things unknown. It gives one a sense of intellectual security to be able to label things and so have them under control, but the idea lives no longer and we, unfortunately, are dead with it. It is the freedom of the myth that gives life-impulse, grace, and poetry, and I have treated this modern fantasy as a myth because it came unhampered from the unconscious. The reduction of such a "myth" of the unconscious to something personal would be harmful and senseless. Such things are the cornerstone for the new building and, amplified by analogy, the meaning is made apparent, otherwise it would be meaningless and, if looked at personalistically, would be quite senseless. Amplified by ancient texts and mysteries one sees afresh the story of the unconscious which adds depth and gives understanding about life, and reveals the roots of our present consciousness.

Naturally, the more archetypal the images, the less they can be associated to the personal life. The archetype is impregnation. It is an innerness or an underlay. It belongs to primordiality while its image can change according to the era. For instance, a train might represent to a modern dreamer what a dragon meant to his ancestors. Actually, getting into an archetypal situation, we get in touch with our ancestors. . . . The archetype, it has been said, is like a river bed deepened by the ages of flowing water. The stream is as life; it changes and renews, and the river bed deepens from the experience and begins to control the river's course. Each flow of water that passes over it is new, but it experiences its flow in accordance with the form of the river bed.

When people have an archetypal experience they feel they have *the* truth, and it is important to be working at something, to be in conscious touch with reality, so that creative ideas can be put into form and life and save us from becoming missionaries. With all great inner experiences there is a danger of cultism. The Eleusinian Mysteries themselves were impregnated with Orphism. Pythagoras reformed Orphism as Orphism had reformed the Dionysion cult. With Pythagoras, in whom there was a shade of other-worldliness, equality was given to woman. "Women as a sex," he wrote, "are more naturally akin to piety." For woman today the task is very difficult; for her world has been divided. Most ancient mysteries were concerned with the problem of dark and light, just the place where any deeper analysis brings us again today. The light and the darkness are in us, and that which has brought us to what we are today weaves the pattern of the future. The inner search means to know the past that the forms of the future become evident.

Feminine psychology has a particular difficulty, for the very bringing of Logos or discrimination to play upon woman's inner life dispels the moonbeams so that they cannot be seen as they really are. Actually it is a place where too much sun can scorch, but if woman is willing to trust herself to the moon's soft light, it can give her understanding even though it renders her speechless. When she understands she understands the piety to which Pythagoras referred, and if she finds inexpressible things she is wiser to be silent. In fact, silence is the only possible thing. In the realm of Eros we arrive at the unutterable. Confrontation with the god cannot be put into words. The veiled god Oannes, who was earlier likened to the old man, had to disappear and discreetly return when it was *right* that he should teach. If a woman has learned anything from her contact, she learns also the wisdom of silence, and the need for the animus to have attributes of the veiled god.[6]

No one can say this or that is the experience, for each individual is in the experience. We can only recognize something of another's experience through our own and not through theirs. Who recognizes Zen but those who have Zen? The individual way reveals a divine mystery to each person, and this according to what he is, and thus reveals the many-faceted nature of the self. Each individual receives from the experience that which is his own, and his relationship to the self. Jung says then: "It is only through the psyche that we can establish that God acts upon us, but we are unable to distinguish whether these actions emanate from God or from the unconscious. We cannot tell whether God and the unconscious are two different entities. Both are borderline concepts for transcendental contents. But empirically it can be established, with a sufficient degree of probability, that there is in the unconscious an archetype of wholeness which manifests itself spontaneously in dreams, etc., and a tendency, independent of the conscious will, to relate other archetypes to this center. Consequently it does not seem improbable that the archetype of wholeness occupies such a central position which approximates it to the God-image. The similarity is further borne out by the peculiar fact that the archetype produces a symbolism which has always characterized and expressed the Deity. These facts make possible a certain qualification of our above thesis

[6] N.B. Many Australian tribes have a cave painting of a human figure with no mouth. The name is Wodgina. No people are more secret than the Australian aborigines about the mysteries which are divulged only on pain of death.

concerning the indistinguishableness of God and the unconscious.

"Strictly speaking the God-image does not coincide with the unconscious as such, but with a special content of it, namely the archetype of the self. It is this archetype from which we can no longer distinguish the God-image empirically. We can arbitrarily postulate a difference between these two entities, but that does not help us at all. On the contrary it only helps us to separate man from God, and prevents God from becoming man. Faith is certainly right when it impresses on man's mind and heart how infinitely far away and inaccessible God is; but it also teaches his nearness and immediate presence, and it is just this nearness which has to be empirically real if it is not to lose all its significance. Only that which acts on me do I recognize as real and actual. But that which has no effect on me might as well not exist. The religious need longs for wholeness, and therefore lays hold on the images of wholeness offered by the unconscious, which, independently of the conscious mind, rise up from the depths of our psychic nature." [7]

As we have seen, such symbols have emerged in the fantasy, a growth from participation mystique to a more conscious state, for in the fifth model the woman is within the circle of water as in the beginning the old man was in the center of the lake. As he was a symbol of timelessness she has come into a sense of timelessness or eternity on a conscious level. As mermaid she was the latent possibility of a self; as woman by the tree she was the self redeemed from its hidden existence. Such work is accompanied by the feeling of immortality which the archetype of the self bestows. Symbols relating to the self and spontaneously manifesting themselves, Jung has noticed, often brought with them a sort of timelessness from the unconscious, expressed in a feeling of eternity. This work conforms to Jung's discoveries and speaks, as it were, out of the eternal or immortal nature of things.

At a place where the human being can allow freedom of expression to the inner voice, a voice which speaks from the depths with none of our conscious concepts or sense of mortality, and can do this without rational interference, he faces indeed his deeper reality which brings with it a feeling of immortality. When

[7] C. G. Jung, *Answer to Job*, page 177.

we consider the fantasy, we see in another way that which existed before ego and that which goes beyond ego and points to ultimate but unknown things. It is as if one is not only this but also that which transcends him. In such a way we come to a knowledge of Nature as she is and have touched upon that which underlies the phenomenal world.

"If you can train yourself to the point of being able to experience psychical contents as objective, then you can feel a psychical presence, for then you know that the psychical contents are not things you have made. They occur, and so you are not alone in the psychical world. You can be perfectly good company, most entertaining company, if you will train yourself to take such things as objective. . . . The experience of the objective fact is all-important, because it denotes the presence of something which is not I, yet is still psychical. Such an experience can reach a climax where it becomes an experience of God. Even the smallest experience of that kind has a mana quality, a divine quality. It is fascinating. A bit more and it is the whole Deity, the giver of life. It is a decisive experience. . . ." [8]

Through the dramatic encounter with these archetypes, we understand more clearly the patterns and the emotions which we live. We glimpse the basis of the mystery of consciousness. In this way we go beyond time and space, and as the center of consciousness moves over, we move from the limitation of the ego into the immortal drama. This is the borderline that prepares the way of physical passing.

In presenting this material, I realize I present but one section of a long process, yet it again illustrates the "way." What happens for the individual who has taken this way is his own personal experience. That one cannot present at all, for he alone is in the experience. Nevertheless I hope I have shown that in such material one can find the underlay which not only affects but which directs life. When one watches the unfolding of a personal myth one must be aware that it is the shaping of a destiny. What is done with it is always individual. Jung has said: "Nobody can know what ultimate things are. We must therefore take them as we experience them. And if such experiences help to make your life

[8] C. G. Jung, *Visions*.

healthier, more beautiful, more complete, and more satisfactory to yourself and those you love, you may safely say, 'This was the grace of God.' " [9]

When the analysand was writing her fantasy, she mentioned that the old man seemed to have been for all time. She referred to him as "Boundless Time." [10] This fact made her analyst suggest she read in Hastings' *Religion and Ethics*, *On the Persian Zarvan Akarana*. This was the God from whom all mankind proceeded. The Zarvanite Sect of Parsiism derived both Ahriman (good spirit) and Ormazd (evil spirit) from Boundless Time. It was not until years later, when the analysand had done a great deal of analogical work on her material, that she read Jung's *Aion*, then published in English. Aion, while being a segment of time, is also Boundless infinite Time. "Aion creates and destroys all things, he is lord and master of the four elements that comprise the universe, and he may be identified with Destiny." [11] What the writer had been realizing was now more clear. The old man was a symbol of the creativity inherent in Time, a principle underlying transformation from the beginnings to modern man. He, the old man, is the infinite, governing and transforming each particular both historically and individually. It is Boundless Time whose transforming process of today creates tomorrow.

He, "the Old Man of the Sea," is also the psychopomp, the leader of the soul, he is the one knowing the whereabouts of the "Treasure" and is thus the able guide. . . . An idea conforming to the central idea of the scriptures.

[9] C. G. Jung, *Psychology and Religion: West and East*, page 114.
[10] See page 33.
[11] E. A. Bennet, *C. G. Jung*, page 115.

CHAPTER 11

An Example of Active Imagination
Following a Recurring Dream

IN THIS piece of Active Imagination I have chosen a theme which has to do with the animus. It, like the previous one, is an extract from a longer piece of work. The analysand had met the animus figure strolling around with a book fastened across his forehead. He told her he represented the "accumulated knowledge of the world," and that he had much to give and no one ever paused to listen. The patient volunteered to come and learn from him. She drew a picture of this very sober person. Before continuing her work with him she began to realize she had contacted an animus figure at whom she would have to look a little more closely.[1] You will notice that, unlike the previous fantasy, the patient entered directly into the dialectic approach and became engaged in the process as an active participant in the drama itself. She wrote:

" 'Manus, would you sit on that chair opposite me? I must know what you are like. I would like to ask you to come on a journey with me, but I would have to be able to recognize you. Are you really this old man with the beard, or do you have some other form?' I waited awhile and he did not reply. 'Yes,' I said, 'I know you are this old man, and I perceive the book on your forehead. I wish you had not that book, for I would like to see you without it.'

"That brought a reply from him. 'You have put it there yourself,' he replied, 'and only you can take it off.'

[1] This work was referred to in Chapter 1.

"I was astonished! *'Did* I? Then what is written on it?' I looked carefully at the book. It was a book of rules . . . all those rules which governed my life. I was upset. 'How I would like to be free from them,' I cried. 'Oh, why did I do it?'

" 'You were afraid you might not live up to a certain standard; so I had to carry them around. They are full of your ideals of service and example. The things which have made life rigid for you.'

"I tried to defend myself. I told him I had been perfectly happy to be obedient to these rules, and that I really wanted to live like that. Then I silently contemplated that weighty book.

" 'If I could be allowed to remove that book from your forehead, I am sure we could talk together so much better,' I said. Then I lifted it from his brow and stood holding it, but I could not throw it away. I looked at him. 'I cannot part with them,' I said. 'I am sure I will need them.'

" 'Then let me carry them,' he said. 'If they are carried in the hand instead of on the head they will not have to lead us.'

" 'How handsome you are,' I said. 'For the first time I see you move and smile freely. All the time it must have been the weight of that book that restricted you.'

" 'Yes,' he replied, nodding, 'it certainly has been the weight of the book that has prevented me from smiling.'

"I felt at home with him now and told him of a dream I had, and asked him if he would come to help me find this child. 'I dreamed I was on top of a hill,' I said. 'Looking over the edge of a cliff, I saw a pool of clear water in which there swam a large fish. Beside me was a little boy who slid from the rocks and disappeared below. Sitting perfectly still on top of the hill was an old, old woman who was clad in black and who watched us silently.'

"So it was that Manus and I began our journey to find the boy. We passed by the old witch who was still sitting there and found ourselves on a bank beside a clear stream. We ran along to find an entrance to a cave where we knew the water flowed, but it was barred by a huge rock. Ferns and trees shaded the stream and the banks. Manus crossed over this stream and went ahead, but I had to go back and walk over a bridge, which was a terrific ordeal, as the bridge was narrow and there was nothing to hold on to.

I felt great relief when I was on the other side and also when I had caught up with Manus. We hurried around the side of a hill and found the pool where the fish was. We had approached it from a different direction, and there in front of us was the cave and we could see there were lights within. From the entrance we could see on the left side a cathedral brightly lit. There were priests in a group standing around something which I could not go close enough to see. On the right there were smaller caves, but they were dark and we could see nothing. As we felt we could not go farther, we stood near the entrance and waited. Outside, all was dark except for the light on the surface of the pool. I knew we must have light to proceed, so I looked around and found a cross on the ground. I picked it up and dipped it in the glowing water, from whence it came luminous with silvery light. I knew this was not suitable for my purpose and looked further and found an unlighted torch. This I dipped also into the water. It came out glowing faintly, and I took it and proceeded to that portion of the cave where the darker caves were. Just inside the entrance of the great cave, there were men like gravediggers trying to make a hole in the ground. When the hole was large enough, Manus went over and dropped the book of rules into it and the whole thing was covered over. We turned then to the left side of the large open cave and waited. Gradually the lights brightened in the cathedral, even lighting up the doorways of the dark caves. As we watched, a hole appeared in the space between the cathedral and the small caves. The hole was circular, and as soon as it was complete the priests came running to this center and formed themselves about it, lying on their faces. I realized the water of life which we could not follow from outside was flowing into this cave and onto the pool where the fish was. The priests formed a design like the petals of a flower, and I knew it was my task to continue the pattern and make it whole. I thought of the stars, the spiral, and the serpent which I had drawn on previous occasions and felt their place was here, for it seemed that everything must come together. I saw the pattern forming: first the priests and then the square. After that the open center claimed my attention, and now I saw the spiral was formed by two serpents who reared their heads as if to hold something aloft. In my hand I still held the torch we had used to bury the book of rules, so I set it on top of the serpents. Immediately they collapsed and the torch fell into the water and was extinguished. At this I was utterly astonished, but remembered the illuminated cross which I had left at the entrance. I took it and set it upon the serpents and they carried it securely, holding it aloft. Then came from somewhere the words: 'My grace is sufficient for thee.' "

We always notice in Active Imagination that talking with figures of the unconscious has a humanizing effect on them, a possibility most helpful when dealing with animus and anima figures, for they represent complexes that can attack from behind, as it were. If we try to make conscious contact with them it stops the flux of involuntary fantasy activity which is, often as not, destructive. In relation to this, I had a patient who had the crazy idea that the neighbors were not kindly disposed toward her. She was a foreigner living in the country of her husband, and so she assumed they expected she should have been exactly like them, and since she was not, they regarded her as inferior. It was a whole lot of fantasy wrongly used, and the way to stop such things is to ask why one thinks like that, and then a woman will find the animus is behaving in an absolutely inhuman way. He has taken over the woman's life and thrives on her suffering. Of course every little innocent action from outside, things normally overlooked, becomes a hook onto which the animus could hang his destructive thoughts.

In such a condition one is really possessed by unconscious voices. Active Imagination is a technique by which one can keep constantly in touch with the unconscious; so in a situation where one is disturbed, one can retire and work on it until one can go decently into one's surroundings; whereas if one keeps things tucked away and not understood, one is poisoned by them. If one has a problem with a real person, one does not do Active Imagination about that person. If the other person has been behaving as a wild animal, then take that as the theme. If one has been oneself the wild animal, it is best to have a look at him. In that way the animal no longer has oneself in its grip. One has got some understanding and saved the outside situation from a dose of one's own animus or anima poison, and also saved oneself from the poison. One must always be sure of one's motives, for if one gets into the devil's kitchen one can get into a mischievous condition and even end in disaster, then one is the devil one is associating with. That is a strong reason why the technique is only suitable for people who have had an analysis and know what they are doing.

In the piece of Active Imagination I have just given, the animus was behaving in a most inhuman way in regard to this woman. He does not criticize the outside world as much as he sits continually upon her. He tells her he carries around a book of rules. That is enough to frighten anyone, and in the psyche he frightened her constantly. He told her she had put the book of rules there, and in a way he is right. The possibility of development of such an animus is already within one. On an already inherent possibility the outer circumstances build. She had within her quite a natural religious attitude, but her upbringing and training resulted in animus opinions dominating her life and turning a natural religious way into something arbitrary and cold. At the tender age of ten years she vowed her life to Christ, and while she thought of Christ as the tender Savior, her animus administered the law from his book of rules in such a way that her life was completely rigid. He gave not a jot for her femininity or her human frailty. What it amounted to was that *he* lived life instead of her. He behaved as such an inhuman giant that she was always ill: constant vomiting for twenty-five years, headaches, and an eye difficulty for which her doctors could find no physical cause. When she came to recognize the animus in the psyche she was filled with curiosity. What does he look like without the book on his head? That had a humanizing effect. Instead of accepting him unquestioningly as *the* wisdom, she wanted to see his face. That is both tender and feminine and it must have taken him by surprise, for he had no law to cover over that very human fact. When the animus takes over a woman's life there is no place for her real thinking, her own ego thoughts. Here the ego confronts him out of itself in a simple and uncomplicated way. He agreed to remove the book of rules and admitted they had kept him from smiling. In fact she had been so ill she laughed very little, and the more she suffered, the more she was pushed on by his inexorable idealistic demands. Such a demanding animus makes it impossible for a woman to find value in her feminine being or to establish some kind of inner truth that is near to her feminine nature. The removal of the book follows a humanizing approach and brings him into conscious existence. Her invitation for him to help her commenced her real activity in regard to him, whereas, previously, she had been forced passively to accept his dictates, not knowing that they differed in any way from her own feminine aim. First we saw that she had to be in a position where she could recognize him. Recognition of the animus is a very necessary step, and it takes tremendous effort on the part of a woman to accomplish this. Therefore to ask to see his face was the primary step in freeing herself from him, or, psychologically, personifying this archetype of the unconscious so that she could free herself from identity with him. Neither men nor women know when they are in the hands of animus or anima, unless they have a means of first separating, and then establishing, a way of recognition.

As the animus figure joins her in the journey she desires to take, they return to the scene brought up in her dream. You will note that she mentions briefly the presence of an old woman. This is the wise old woman, the ancient one who is also a witch, the one whose manipulation of destiny is continuous. It is as if one always knows such a figure to be something divine and also something sinister. This feminine creature is a nature being who weaves the web of life and uses people in a remarkable way. In this piece of work, unlike the last one, the old woman is merely sitting and the writer passes her by. I would think from this Active Imagination that the writer was so intent on her search for the child and the companionship of the animus on a new basis that she was neither drawn to nor afraid of this old, old woman, who was thus able to continue her work in Nature's way. In fairy tales the heroine is often punished for too much curiosity and also for neglect. One is expected to have the right judgment of just how things are wanted by Nature. The heroine is expected to have a feeling finesse, not to ignore yet not to overdo things. Here in this work the writer notices the old woman assumes she is a witch and has not the wrong sort of curiosity toward her, and there seems to be no fear at the contact with such a sinister figure. It would seem that as far as the writer was concerned, the old woman was recognized, but there was no nasty smell attached to the situation. At any rate it was not time for contact with this archetype. She appears perhaps as a test or warning. This is a figure who will come up and demand recognition later on. One always has a certain feeling when watching Active Imagination that things are or are not stated in the right way. The old witch is a tremendously important archetype and one who must not be overlooked, yet here in this place I would say that since she is not interfering with the progress of the patient she should not be interfered with. She will do her work quietly and in her own time become prominent. People in analysis especially have veritable witch hunts and shadow hunts. Darkness is part of Nature; when "she" interferes in the game of life one needs to look at the situation. Otherwise she can be left quietly sitting.

The animus goes ahead crossing over the stream. This is again an archetypal motif. He leads her to the inner world, but does not make the journey for her. The bridge is narrow and there is no handrail, and even though he leads, she has to support herself and rely on her own feminine capacity. This in itself is quite a reversal from the effect he has had on her life. She must be more aware of herself. The crossing over the stream is the moving into another reality, a different time. Thus it leads immediately to the cave, the dwelling of the Great Earth Mother, the positive aspect of the "old witch woman," whom she had contacted earlier. The cave is the feminine world and the place of rebirth to which the animus has led her. That is his positive role; he and the anima in man are the bridge to the unconscious. Here in the womb of life there was no place for the book of rules. Here at the entrance to the cathedral of the inner world stood gravediggers ready to bury such possessions. Here all one's conscious learning and values have no place. As she brought the primitive torch, lit by the waters of the unconscious, the animus made the gesture that buried the rules he had carried so long, thus allowing her to enter the feminine realm unhampered by his peculiar logic. After escorting her to the entrance of this Eros domain he took no more active part. She was now in a world where he must pause and wait. Had he kept possession of the book of rules he might have forced her to stay, but he was leaving her free to go, not only to the feminine world, but also to enter into a different time, for in her attempt at wholeness she faced not only Christian symbols but those valid in all times.

It was not the cross she had to carry in here but rather the fiery torch, and only after that was she ready to see the opposites together. This was the beginning of a new consciousness. For her it was a startling realization, to be followed by the long, long task of assimilation. The work had also a physical effect, for from the time she removed the book from the head of Manus, her continual headaches ceased. The important thing in this type of work is that it opens up a way and it then depends on the individual if he will merely grasp at these things and let them drift again into the unconscious or face the task of assimilating them every day. The lovely petals of a rose are fed from the dark stuffs of the earth. This darkness is transformed into the beauty and the scent of the petals. In the same way man is what he has assimilated, and he has to assimilate the darkness of which he was ignorant, as well as the past which has built his present. The experience which points the way to wholeness must be our daily food; only then can the image lead to some kind of completeness on earth. It requires, too, the right attitude to the work produced. The fantasy is a psychological fact and must be accepted that way. It is a fact affecting life, whether we are conscious of it or not. When people have no opportunity to recognize such facts they constellate outside in one's external surroundings. Jung says: "Myth is not fiction: it consists of facts that are continually repeated and can be observed over and over again. It is something that happens to man, and men have mythical fates just as much as the Greek heroes do. The fact that the life of Christ is largely myth does absolutely nothing to disprove its factual truth—quite the contrary. I would even go so far as to say that the mythical character of a life is just what expresses its universal human validity. It is quite possible, psychologically, for the unconscious or an archetype to take complete possession of a man and to determine his fate down to the smallest detail. At the same time objective, non-psychic phenomena can occur which also repre- sent the archetype. It not only seems so, it simply is so, that the archetype fulfills itself not only psychically in the individual, but objectively outside the individual." [2]

It is such knowledge and seeing how such things work within oneself and their effect on outer life that make unassailable the

[2] C. G. Jung and C. Kerenyi, *Introduction to a Science of Mythology.*

great importance of the work done on one's own psyche. If a woman allows the animus to suppress her, she finds life is suppressing her. Unconsciously she invites the men in her life to behave in exactly the same way as the animus. A man who knows nothing of his anima might find that the women in his surroundings behave exactly as this hidden goddess. And it always looks as if it really is so. When the analyst is faced with the problems of relationship, he looks for the projections in which the patient is caught by these hidden gods of the unconscious. Sometimes it is mainly projection, sometimes the other person comes under the spell of these archetypes and behaves in a way which is really not his own, and it also happens that these archetypes will attract to the patient the very person who can carry these projections so that he or she can live out the fate they determine for them.

In the fantasy we have taken, it is true that this animus figure cut the woman off from life, behaving in a most orthodox and exemplary manner, so that the natural feminine was quite suffocated, and because everything he told her was in fact material that is stressed again and again in the Logos world, she had no way of escape but through what seemed an unjust sickness. To come again to the feminine realm means to face the animus from a new standpoint. St. Augustine said that woman has no soul for she is soul. If a woman has the courage to leave the Logos world and seek and give value to the feminine truth, the animus is her guide and friend. Whole in herself, her sons are free, and she passes to them the mystery of the soul that they, too, may face life.

CHAPTER **12**

Some Questions Answered

AFTER presenting this material to a group of people, certain questions were asked. I have therefore used these questions as my final chapter because they are indeed qustions that could quite naturally be asked again. The answers are an attempt to throw some light on this subject and its relation to "creative art."

Questions asked and answered

Question: Even though you say Active Imagination is brought about by the conscious attitude to the unconscious, which calls forth and allows freedom of imagery, etc., the result seems to me to smack of the spontaneous eruptions common to the creative artist and inspired person. For hunches and inspiration we are dependent on complexes, yet you say we cannot reduce the artistic creation to a symptom. If it comes from a complex, isn't it symptomology? Isn't the "inspiratrix" a symptom?

Answer: It is true that we depend on complexes. Complexes are not necessarily a pathological sign. When a complex is too powerful, too overcharged, it can have a disturbing effect on consciousness. Like every value, it has a negative possibility also. And that negative side is also revealed in the process of Active Imagination. Behind your question it seems there is a confusion between the personal and non-personal aspect of the complex. The personal aspect of the complex is surely the repressed or subliminal content. However, it has also a non-personal element in the archetype. You spoke of the "inspiratrix" and ask is she a symptom? I suppose you mean a symptom of the personal mother complex. On one hand, yes, but in that form is more limited, less universal in appeal, and less *the* inspiratrix. The anima, for example, can wear the clothes of the personal mother, but she is much more than that; she is an archetype as old as consciousness itself. In that form she is the fountain of inspiration of a universal nature which transcends the personal unconscious as all mythologies reveal. When her tongue speaks, her words, whether sinister or hallowed, are moving, profound, because the voice is impersonal, and since her words are true for all times, they are awarded the hallmark of true inspiration.

Question: I am still a little at sea about the complex. For example, I can see how I could have a mother complex and, as a result, have an anima with qualities of my mother, and I can understand from experience how I can project these qualities. But how can I, as an individual, have any contact with a non-personal attribute of my anima? How would she get such non-personal attributes?

Answer: Probably the key is in the fact that you said "my anima." The anima is an archetype of the collective unconscious. She is the Great Mother since the dawn of time. Man inherits, not something static like the image of a primordial mother, but an image-forming potential by which she is revealed again and again in many ways. Dr. Neumann's book *The Great Mother* gives an idea of the magnitude of this. The personal mother, in her all-powerful role when a child is young, is naturally clothed by the child's fantasy in supra-personal robes. As he develops, she recedes as the divine heroine and becomes more human. When *the* anima is seen *only* in the clothes of the personal mother, the personal mother is invested with the role of the archetype. Therefore when she inspires it has a more personal flavor and is much less the voice of the universal Great Mother.

Question: Yet behind that is the Universal Anima or soul, who, if she is not steel-bound by the trappings of the personal mother, can inspire one from Universal Wisdom. In which case it is the voice of the Symbol which speaks and not that of a symptom. Is that right?

Answer: Yes.

Question: Then is not all creative art a form of Active Imagination? Also since creative imagination is part of a therapeutic process, should not the artist be the most developed and adapted personality, which he obviously isn't from general standards?

Answer: I will attempt to answer your question in the sequence in which you have presented it.

There are many works that clearly fall into the framework of Active Imagination. Such works as Goethe's *Faust*, Nietzsche's *Zarathustra*, Melville's *Moby Dick*, and Jack London' *Red One* are a few examples. Professor Jung himself has written a great deal on Goethe's *Faust* and he gave seminars on *Zarathustra*. Dr. Kirsch of Los Angeles has lectured on both *Moby Dick* and the *Red One*. In all these works the unconscious is allowed freedom while the conscious selects and adds to the over-all structure. From Dr. Kirsch's *Moby Dick* lectures, which were privately circulated in 1957, I would like to quote: "Let us pause here for a moment and consider the extraordinary courage which Melville demonstrated by starting the journey on that ocean which we now call the unconscious. He was truly a modern man. He discovered the unconscious as a psychological fact and understood its psychological significance, its effect on the human being, and in this way he also discovered the process of individuation for himself. We, in our daily analytical work, are, and must be, aware of the fact that in touching the unconscious, and especially in activating imagination, enormous forces are released in our patients. They can be employed for good or evil, frequently for both. Although many other factors are involved, the outcome depends largely on the purity of the intention. In the end a confrontation with the self, an 'Auseinandersetzung,' must occur, and our patients are already strongly pushed by their complexes or their neuroses before they seek the human help of the modern medicine man. Creative writers and artists especially are often somewhere in mid-ocean when they seek our help; frequently they are already foundering in a furious storm! But Melville had no analyst to consult. He was alone in the America of the nineteenth century and even his best and true friend Hawthorne wondered why he was so possessed with the idea of God. In his day and age it was an utterly lonely trip which significantly began on Christmas Day. That is to a large degree, it was a departure from his essentially Christian consciousness. In our day, after two World Wars and with thermonuclear reactions threatening the very life of mankind, many more have started such a journey, even though we surely do not know exactly where our own journey will end." [1] The artist embarks on his journey alone. He clings to the land or returns to it by his critical approach to his own creation. This gives him some security, even if he is aware at the time that the material is beyond his ego concepts.

Now certain creative works can be, as we have said earlier, symptomatic. Some works express disturbances of the personal unconscious, that area of the psyche made up of repressions and material available more or less readily to consciousness. A great work of art springs from deeper levels, and here we find the symbolic works. When we begin to analyze such a work, we must be careful not to reduce the artist to a symptom, for if we do that, nothing of importance has been gained and we have missed something very valuable. For instance, what have we said if we point out an artist's father or mother complex? Is it saying that his creative genius can be equated with a rash on his chin? Jung, in his analysis of a symbolic work, gives fullest value to the genius of the self and is aware of the artist's attempts at individuation. To reduce a work of art purely to the personal sphere does not give proper value to the symbols used. Biological causality, while justified in some measure when applied to man, cannot be applied to creative art itself.

"When, for example, Plato expresses the whole problem of the theory of cognition in his metaphor of the cave, or when Christ expresses the idea of the Kingdom of Heaven in his parables, these are genuine and true symbols; namely, attempts to express a thing, for which there exists as yet no adequate verbal concept. If we were to interpret Plato's metaphor in the manner of Freud we should naturally come to the uterus, and we should have proved that even the mind of Plato was deeply stuck in the primeval levels of 'infantile sexuality.' But in doing so we should also remain in total ignorance of what Plato actually created from the primitive antecedents of his philosophical intuition; we should, in fact, carelessly have overlooked his most essential product, merely to discover that he had 'infantile' fantasies like every other mortal. Such a conclusion could possess

[1] James Kirsch, *The Enigma of Moby Dick*, page 4.

value only for the man who regards Plato as a superhuman being, and who is therefore able to find a certain satisfaction in the fact that even Plato was also a man. But who would want to regard Plato as a god? Surely only a man who is afflicted by the tyranny of infantile fantasies, in other words, a neurotic mentality. For such a one the reduction to universal human truths is profitable on medical grounds. But this would have nothing whatever to do with the meaning of the Platonic parable." [2]

"Before analytical psychology can do justice to the work of art it must entirely rid itself of medical prejudice; for the art work is not morbidity and therefore demands a wholly different orientation from the medical. The physician must naturally seek the prime cause of a sickness in order to eradicate it, if possible, by the roots; but just as naturally must the psychologist adopt an exactly opposite attitude toward the work of art. He will not raise the question, which for the art work is quite superfluous, concerning its undoubted general antecedents, its basic human determinants; but he will inquire into the meaning of the work, and will be concerned with its preconditions only in so far as they are necessary for the understanding of its meaning. Personal causality has as much and as little to do with the work of art as the soil with the plant that springs from it. Doubtless we may learn to understand some peculiarities of the plant by becoming familiar with the character of its habitat. And for the botanist this is, of course, an important component of his knowledge. But nobody will maintain that he has thereby recognized all the essentials relating to the plant itself. The personal orientation that is demanded by the problem of personal causality is out of place in the presence of the work of art, just because the work of art is not a human being, but essentially supra-personal." [3]

Great works of art seem as if a "being" has used the artist as a creative medium. Of course the medium is not universally identical, for some people, when they create, are consciously in control. That is, they organize and manipulate words, material, etc., because they have the end production in mind. There is no difference between them and the creative urge. Such people never are astounded at their own productions. On the other hand, others

[2] C. G. Jung, *Contributions to Analytical Psychology*, page 232.
[3] Ibid., page 233.

are overtaken by the creative idea, they feel compelled, often exhausted, and are amazed and delighted at the achieved result. These people are often aware that they are instruments in the hands of an impulse beyond themselves. "Practical analysis of artists invariably shows not only the strength of the creative impulse springing from the unconscious, but also its splenetic and arbitrary character. We have only to turn to any of the biographies of the great artists to find abundant evidence of the way in which the creative urge works upon them; often it is so imperious that it actually absorbs every human impulse, yoking everything to the service of the work, even at the cost of health and common human happiness. The unborn work in the soul of the artist is a force of nature that effects its purpose, either with tyrannical might, or with that subtle cunning which Nature brings to the achievement of her end, quite regardless of the personal weal or woe of the man who is the vehicle of the creative force. The creative energy lives and waxes in the man as a tree in the earth from which it takes its nourishment. It might be well, therefore, to regard the creative process as a living thing, implanted, as it were, in the souls of men. In terms of analytical psychology this is an autonomous complex. It is in fact a detached portion of the psyche that leads an independent psychic life withdrawn from the hierarchy of consciousness, and, in proportion to its energic value or force, may appear as a mere disturbance of the voluntarily directed process of consciousness, or as a super-ordinated authority which may take the ego bodily into its service. The latter case, therefore, would be the poet who is identified with the creative process and who at once acquiesces whenever the unconscious 'must' threatens. But the other poet to whom the creative element appears almost as a foreign power is unable for one reason or another to acquiesce, and is, accordingly, caught by the 'must' unawares." [4]

It always seems to me that when we look at any work of art, we can't distinguish the process unless we know the personality. Even then it is difficult, for both attitudes can govern a person at different times. The whole and deep significance of a symbolic work of art can be lost to consciousness when it is made to conform to tradition and is appreciated merely as a work of art.

[4] Ibid., pages 238ff.

"In order to convert it from a purely aesthetic interest into a living reality it must also reach life and be accepted and live in the sphere of reality." [5] That is the attempt of Active Imagination, to bring it in its livingness into the world, regardless of prescribed or traditional form.

That brings us to your second point. There is a definite connection between the artistic creation and Active Imagination. However, Active Imagination makes no claim to being a finished piece of work. The participant, by turning consciously to the unconscious, is doing what the creative artist does, but his intention is perhaps more conscious. Whereas the artist develops his creative work to present it to others, the participant in Active Imagination has a goal, freedom for the unconscious to reveal itself. He strives consciously after wholeness of personality. What it means to himself is the prime importance of the venture. I would suggest you read Jung's chapter entitled "Poetic Art" in *Contributions to Analytical Psychology*.

As to whether the poet should be the most adapted and when he is obviously not more so than others, this question can only be answered this way: There is a difference between adaptation and adjustment. The artist is an educator. He seizes upon unconscious images, presents them in a form that makes them acceptable to at least some of his contemporaries. He might touch material that future people will appreciate because his voice is beyond his time. He brings to the surface the thoughts of his time which have not been accepted into the general conscious atmosphere. Therefore the really creative artist is one who walks lonely, frightening, inspiring byways. His journey is not along the safe highways of collective thinking. To the highway he returns to bring at least a glimpse of his find when he himself beats new paths in the wilderness. Thus he lives somewhat in two worlds. He can't, like the average man, walk exclusively on the highway. If he were thoroughly adjusted to the general atmosphere, he would not yearn after the byways and the wilderness and the uncharted seas. However, the process of finding and refining means that he makes an attempt at individuation. He has two worlds, not one, and the conflict, so long as he can bear it and use it, is a matrix of creative energy.

[5] C. G. Jung, *Psychological Types*, page 228.

However, the person who does Active Imagination is not thereby an individuated person. His advantage is the awareness of his attempt. You will recall that at the beginning of the book I mentioned that after the analysis of personal material one is not left bereft, that a new center arises from the unconscious, and that this center is superior to the ego. You see one cannot term it "I," nor can one regard it as a "shadow" of the ego. Whichever way one looks at this new center one finds it is superior. Who then, we ask, is this center? Here at last is the self of whom we speak so much. To experience this self is a transforming experience. To live life really fully leads one naturally from the ego to the self and is, in fact, the individuation process. Now to make such a discovery via Active Imagination does not necessarily mean that this is an individuated person. The work says more or less in symbolic language "this is your way." That way is always unique and individually understood. The advantage of Active Imagination is that one is then more conscious of the "way" if the material is understood.

Question: Then if the creative artist were able to regard his material as the participant in Active Imagination does, he would discover much that would be of benefit to his own personality, is that so?

Answer: Yes. Such a work as Nietzsche's *Zarathustra* presented Nietzsche's conflict. On one hand the wise old man and on the other the shadow or inferior man. Nietzsche could not accept the inferior man. Had an analyst been on the spot he might more readily have acknowledged both sides and been saved an inflation by the wise old man, a condition which led to all his misery.

Question: The Active Imagination given seems to me, quite apart from the analogous material explaining its connection with collective motifs throughout the ages, to have quite an impact as a religious experience. Yet it is not an orthodox Christian religious experience—in fact it has something pagan in it. Has an inner experience of this nature, assuming my assumption is right, any connection with orthodoxy?

Answer: Yes, I would say so, but in that it expresses something of inner experiences out of which religions emanate. The word "orthodox" suggests things must "be" in a certain way. When one has an outward form of religion, the whole thing can be projected, God is completely outside. There is no inward experience of God. That is, one doesn't have inner personal experience. People can be orthodox Christians and within the psyche be pagan, as a Western world proves when the forces of evil are swamping our Christian world. Jung said: "So long as religion is only faith and outward form, and the religious function is not experienced in our own souls, nothing of any importance has happened. It has yet to be understood that the 'mysterium magnum' is not only an actuality but is first and foremost rooted in the human psyche. The man who does not know this from his own experience may be a most learned theologian, but he has no idea of religion and still less of education." [6] It is necessary to know that great religious experience, the great mystery itself, is rooted in the human psyche. Unless one knows this, for all one's religious conforming, one can be ignorant, in the true meaning of religion. You are quite right to intuit the work as having a religious impact; you are concerned because it leads to what is easily recognized as Christian and you see its connection with pagan cults. It is an experience of the psyche extending over the ages, it touches again, with impact, that which has molded all great religions of the world. It shows again the need for inner experience in our Christian world if Christianity is to live again. Psychology is not bound by creed. Jung says: "Not everyone possesses the spiritual strength of a Tertullian. It is evident not only that he had the strength to sustain paradoxes but that they actually afforded him the highest degree of religious certainty. The inordinate number of spiritual weaklings makes paradoxes dangerous. So long as the paradox remains unexamined and is taken for granted as a customary part of life, it is harmless enough. But when it occurs to an insufficiently cultivated mind (always, as we know, the most sure of itself) to make the paradoxical nature of some tenet of faith the object of its lucubrations, as earnest as they are impotent, it is not long before such a one will break out into iconoclastic and scornful laughter, pointing to the manifest absurdity of the mystery. Things have gone rapidly downhill since the Age of Enlightenment, for, once this petty reasoning mind, which cannot endure any paradoxes, is awakened, no sermon on earth can keep it down. A new task then arises: to

[6] C. G. Jung, *Psychology and Alchemy*, page 12.

lift this still undeveloped mind step by step to a higher level and to increase the number of persons who have at least some inkling of the scope of paradoxical truth. If this is not possible, then it must be admitted that the spiritual approaches to Christianity are as good as blocked. We simply do not understand any more what is meant by the paradoxes contained in dogma; and the more external our understanding of them becomes the more we are affronted by their irrational form, until finally they become completely obsolete, curious relics of the past. The man who is stricken in this way cannot estimate the extent of his spiritual loss, because he has never experienced the sacred images as his own psychic structure. But it is just this indispensable knowledge that the psychology of the unconscious can give him, and its scientific objectivity is of the greatest value here. Were psychology bound to a creed it would not and could not allow the unconscious of the individual that free play which is the basic condition for the production of archetypes. It is precisely the spontaneity of archetypal contents that convinces, whereas any prejudiced intervention is a bar to genuine experience. If the theologian really believes in the almighty power of God on the one hand and in the validity of dogma on the other, why then does he not trust God to speak in the soul? Why this fear of psychology? Or is, in complete contradiction to dogma, the soul itself a hell from which only demons gibber? Even if this were really so it would not be any the less convincing; for as we all know the horrified perception of the reality of evil has led to at least as many conversions as the experience of good." [7]

Question: Do you see any significance in the woman being contacted by an artist rather than any other man who could have involved her on the human level? Why does he paint her portrait? Is this vanity or would that be too much an assumption of ego?

Answer: As I see it the woman had taken the journey of descent. The portraits could have been an attempt to make permanent the glimpse the artist caught of the "other" world, as it were. A portrait often has a sort of divine essence which speaks of something beyond that human being. I would suggest that the painting itself was an act which held onto the spirit—the spirit which ultimately enabled her to escape from being totally in the

[7] Ibid., page 16.

world "below," and to seek again the jewel she lost. Perhaps that was the artist's positive function, even though he stole the jewel, as it were, with his left hand. By the positive act, the theft was doomed to failure but had to be experienced. Could we say that on the level in which we are interpreting this A.I., the portrait represents vanity? If so this is also part of falling into "Egypt" which is the core of the whole thing, the going down and the return. I brought the analogy of the Poem of the Pearl regarding this. Active Imagination is a picture on many levels, descent and involvement being necessary steps in development. It is the path of individuation. The human psyche does descend from its original "oneness," depart from its primal quest by being absorbed into the material world, and only then finds its way back to the source. It is however the ineffable core which never relinquishes its hold that makes the journey possible at all. I have tried to show this as a myth of the unconscious projected via Active Imagination. The dreamer is not an ego per se, but a figure in this internal drama.

Question: It strikes me, as a lecturer in English, that a sexual problem is implied here. Can you say something about this?

Answer: Sexual symbolism is used in the humanizing aspect, the involvement in this world, and also to express the involvement with her "creator." Actually it was not indicating such a problem, and if it were it would not be the essence of the whole exercise. I think you are falling into the error so many people do, looking for a symptom instead of the import of the whole thing. This limits understanding. Have the gods not always slept with man?

Question: The figure "Wisdom" is regarded as an archetype. Would the participant feel in a case like this that he or she had a special claim on Wisdom in life?

Answer: You are wondering if a person who confronted such a figure would get an inflation and grab it as an ego quality. That is always a possibility and a danger; that is why I emphasized that it is necessary to get back to the objective nature of the psyche and also the collective aspect of such figures. It seems as if one has to be at first gripped by such a figure, then when one's human ordinariness awakens, something of the aroma of the archetype possibly clings to one.

Question: How does one know that that figure "Wisdom" is *really* great wisdom?

Answer: That is never claimed. She is an archetypal image. The figure suggests there is a deep wisdom in Nature, that there is a Divine Wisdom. The archetypal image points to something beyond. That is her numinous role. She *represents* ultimate wisdom. There is no metaphysical statement in this. It would be indeed foolish to say, "This is how Wisdom looks or behaves." The Mother Goddess or Divine Wisdom was represented in this way in this particular piece of work. From analogy we find she is represented in many ways—all ways old and new revealing the archetype.

Question: You said Active Imagination is not a simple technique although it looks simple on the surface. I have been wondering why it is dangerous to do Active Imagination. Could you tell us how the analyst can help to keep the process a safe medium for analytic use?

Answer: An analyst who uses this method must really understand it, and the only way to understand it is to experience it in one's own analysis. It is more than letting the story of the unconscious take form. It is of vital importance to know what is happening and along what lines the material is unfolding. One must never lose sight of the fact that it is the structural underlay of life and that the course which leads to wholeness leads both up and down. The values of the unconscious are not the values of ordinary rational life. The analyst must know when to say something and when to remain silent, for a patient will always want something to be said, and always at a place where it is important he should know for himself. When it comes to amplification, this should be done by the analysand himself. It has more effect than anything an analyst could say, although the analyst with his wider knowledge can explain and point out analogical material. Arbitrary opinions never help. And too much intellectualism can ruin the whole process. Therefore the amplifications done should be faced with an open mind and a sincere and devoted attitude. That does not mean there should be no criticism and that everything which presents itself as analogy should be swallowed whole. Once the purposive nature of the psyche is realized, whatever enlargements are done are better than explanation. An analyst's awareness of his own unconscious has meaning for the analysand who feels understood while he is finding his way in uncharted seas.

Now here is a very important thing; the analyst's personal experience with the hinterland of his own psyche protects him from being involved in the patient's material. When one touches archetypal material it can, because of its universal appeal and validity, be fascinating. The analyst can't help being changed a little by it, but he must not be drawn into it. So he does not discuss it until the patient has established his own point of view. Every analysis is a completely new situation, and that's the art, to let it be unique, to be in it with the patient and out of it and objective about it at the same time.

There is no absolute example of what Active Imagination should be. To be influenced by someone else's work never brings one to one's own truth. Therefore it is not good for an analysand to read or absorb the material of another person. The safety of the participant rests in the experience and integrity of the analyst. If he has faced the unconscious without being dissolved in it and brought back values to consciousness, he is aware of the dangers. He will understand symbols leading to wholeness which, added to consciousness, have a deepening and widening effect on the personality. He also can see the dangers where no center seems forthcoming, or can we say that there is no thread but a fragmentation. This is where he needs all his knowledge and the means of closing off such potential dangers.

The patient must retain his previous values and enlarge them. To be taken over by the archetypal images means moving from "fitness to unfitness." Therein lies the therapeutic responsibility.

Creative activity itself is something that has been recognized in man from time immemorial, so also have we recognized the artists' use of symbolism. However, the psychological background of such creative activity becomes more clear through revelations of analytical psychology and is especially obvious in Active Imagination wherein the unconscious psyche is given full scope in the use of symbolism. As you have seen from the material presented, it is a symbolism naïvely and simply used, but revealing truths transcending the participating ego and stretching out to touch once again those symbols which have "always been."

Question: There is a question I would like to ask which has not to do with Active Imagination as such. It is this. You spoke of a man (and woman in a reverse case) expecting of a woman to be feminine in a way that he sees femininity. Is this picture he has of the feminine being actually a picture of his own anima which he wants to see lived out by his wife?

Answer: Yes, that is so. He can be convinced that that is the way she should be, and so strong is the image that he does not accept the wife's individual reality. Of course when he falls in love he projects much of that image onto her. She must have some hook for such a projection. However, as long as this works one is not in doubt, and therefore it is only possible to speak of it as a projection when the inner image and the outer reality do not agree. Then only is one in doubt as to who the other person really is. Then in the case of the anima, it nudges the man along to demand his wife step into line with the anima image. The same is true of a woman's animus. The thing that has worked for young people when in love often fails to work as they mature and develop individual status. The process of maturity is to recognize the other as he or she is. It is impossible to change the process of individuation.

Question: This leads me to another question regarding the first fantasy. The Old Man we have seen is an archetypal motif. Now is this a projection of the animus of the writer?

Answer: In a sense, yes. She had turned outside for learning and wisdom. I would say she had a "bearded animus." Through the experience and impact of the work done in Active Imagination she began to accept that the archetypes function through herself and to accept responsibility for the "child." No longer did the world fascinate her. She had comparisons from within. In this way people walk on surer ground.

Question: Now may I carry this further for clarification? The Old Man is more or less equated with the Deity in the interpretation. You speak of him also as an animus figure. Are the two interpretations compatible?

Answer: With such a work we see it from many levels. The

animus in his highest aspect has a divine quality. The Old Man is the transformed animus, a figure akin to Wisdom. In the story we followed the transforming process. In the beginning he kept the woman unconscious and in captivity (a particularly frequent activity of the animus). Then he became the highest concept; the Old Man who inspires but departs and no longer keeps the woman captive. You also saw the need of the "woman" to be active in this drama. Thus the story reveals the individuation process of woman. Coming from the unconscious, it hints at the "way." So you see the Old Man also represents the old and outgrown animus.

Question: In relation to painters, do you consider artistic works are representations of the unconscious?

Answer: Yes, great works. Artists often portray such things that their contemporaries are shocked about. Take, for instance, Breughel's paintings. In his picture of Christ's Journey to Calvary, in the distance Christ carries his cross, while in the foreground people do not look; they gamble and laugh and ignore the whole thing. Another picture shows the Temptation of St. Anthony. The latter picture influenced Flaubert to write his erudite work on the *Temptations of St. Anthony.* This book, like Breughel's painting, foretells the future where man turns from spiritual to a materialistic age. The change was already working in the unconscious of people, and the artist, in touch with unconscious urges, portrays it. Flaubert was told his manuscript should be destroyed. No one wanted anything to do with it. Breughel was a controversial figure. Looking back, we can see what was happening. For them, and many great artists like them, it meant a clash with public opinion and the suffering which accompanied it. All art does not speak of the future. Some stretches back as if to bring the unconscious closer. It seems like an attempt to reinforce consciousness from below so that the split will not be too great. One does not ask the artist about the meaning of his work. For him it is a matter of putting his thoughts into color and line. He does not interpret it psychologically. Even though the artist might think he chooses his subjects, he is, in fact, gripped by an idea. The idea works on him. He might say, "I paint sea nymphs because I am interested in sea nymphs." Why he has this interest is not important. The fact is, the idea has caught him and he is interested because he is caught, therefore his creative powers are called forth. The artist produces a symbolic expression of the archetypes working in his time. Work without a message is never a living work, however deftly accomplished. Art is a serious business expressing the deeper meaning of life itself.

Question: You have said the "self" for a woman is feminine and for a man, masculine. You said also that the unconscious and conscious combination make the self. In the unconscious of an ego the opposite sex exists. Can you explain this apparent anomaly?

Answer: I will try. The idea of the self is a way of looking at the ideal of wholeness. We do not know what the self is. We see symbolic references to wholeness. Suppose we say the ego relation to the self is as a small circle within a large one. As we enlarge consciousness, we know more of the larger one. But the more we know of the larger one, the further its boundaries are removed. In other words we denote by a large circle what we mean by the self, whereas it is, as far as we are concerned, boundaryless. Woman finds in the self the principle of femininity and man finds the principle of masculinity. But these are a pair. They are the divine syzygy. So the self is both. The self is a many faceted concept. It is a way of conceiving a difficult thing, but is not something static. It is dark and light, great and small, male and female. The individuation process has to do with the syzygy that is within man and woman. Symbols of the self have a uniting character.

Question: It is clear to me that Active Imagination is not an easy process. What do you consider are some of the greatest difficulties one encounters in an attempt to do it?

Answer: Well, first, as I have said, the art of being simple is in itself a difficulty for our Western way of thinking. Secondly, it seems to me the attitude of the animus and anima is highly important. You see, the animus and anima have the greatest tendency to distort things. When one does Active Imagination they are likely to distort until the whole thing seems stupid or artificial and not worth proceeding with. To imprison the animus and anima is difficult, yet it is the art of just letting things happen, of learning reality in this way, which has an imprisoning effect on them. In daily life nothing stops the animus and anima intervention so surely as facing facts just as they are, no opinions, no moods. You see, the animus and anima throw a veil over reality and then facts look like something else. Theoretically it sounds easy enough, but when these devils have one by the neck it is the most difficult task to depotentialize them. I have found that doing this task in Active Imagination, that is, following the art of letting things happen, helps one to do likewise in daily life. When the animus and anima have had things their own way for a long time without question or hindrance, to take up the task of excluding them in favor of reality seems like doing violence to one's dearest relation. That is something we have to stand. I will illustrate from a life situation. The interference of animus and anima seems easier to recognize there. A man, whose wife had an opinionating animus who talked frightful nonsense, was in analysis. He would go home to find the animus talking all sorts of stuff. Some sounded all right but didn't fit the facts at all. So he would try to straighten it out and the animus would twist and come in from another direction until he would retire in a terrible mood and be quite exhausted. Then, of course, he would complain to me. I tried to get him to retire from such discussions, read his newspaper, anything, in order to see the effect this would have on the wife's animus. He was feeding this lion a hearty meal when he got entangled. To leave meant the animus would be starved out. But no, his anima loved to get him into it even though he suffered. He would rationalize the thing saying there had been a few times when he felt he'd done a good job sorting it all out for her; that it was very thrilling when he did. So his anima dangled that before his nose so that he could not see the fact that now she (the anima) really loved to be in all this nonsense even if it ended in a hellish business for both of them. The fact was, nine times out of ten it ended badly, but the anima would not allow him to be willing to try to withdraw. It was doing violence to her. One has to do such violence to succeed. One has to be willing to be the cruel one until one has the anima or animus doing her or his work properly. Only then can one afford to enter such a situation. So you see how difficult it is. People will go through hell rather than give up possession by the animus or anima. It is just the same when a woman has to give up her animus opinions and see facts as they are. One woman had an idea she had no feeling. (Now that is never true. One can have inferior feeling, feeling that is difficult to even recognize, but it is buried there somewhere.) However, she decided, or her animus decided, she must use feminine feeling, so she took up all sorts of occupations in charity work, acted in such and such a way according to his opinions, and thought she was living the thing. One must give her credit for a heroic attempt, but the fact was she was animus possessed. Feeling is an evaluating function. She did not ask herself how she felt until the day came when she could stand it all no longer and was able to look at facts. Challenging the animus and anima is not easy. It results in a new situation, a situation which is always difficult, for those two do not take kindly to control, therefore the attempt is beset by an onslaught from them. It seems as if everything in one's surroundings tempts one to become their victim again. Now in the same way, one's Active Imagination comes under fire from the animus and anima until one learns to disentangle and accept the work quite simply, even naïvely.

Question: You spoke of animus and anima doing their work properly. What, when they are divested of negativism, is their "proper work"? We so often malign them because the negative aspect is the easiest to see.

Answer: The animus as discrimination, spiritual guide, the anima as understanding with qualities of relatedness are a divine pair. They are part of the make-up of mankind and essential to the wholeness of the human being. I agree with you that because their negative aspect so often causes us trouble one is inclined to hear them more often maligned than praised. However if you will read Jung's own discussion of them in *Aion* you will recognize them as psychopomps. They are not inventions of the conscious. They are, as Jung says "spontaneous products of the unconscious." They are archetypes which have tremendous influence on the conscious. The anima links man with reality and the animus links woman with her spiritual nature. They hold hands with the inner and the outer world and lead to wholeness.

Question: The drame intérieur which you have set forth for us has its roots in the beginnings and leads to futurity as all mythology seems to do. We are coming more and more to recognize there is in us a man a million years old. This, of course, is paralleled by the biological man. Have you been aware of this connection?

Answer: Actually, I know very little indeed about biological man. However, it is claimed that the brain itself incorporates the whole history of evolution, from the small sea anemone-like beginnings to the development of a "new" brain—the cortex—which has to do with the outer world. This new brain controls impulses, etc. It is "social" in its function. The brain, from conception to when a child is born, goes through every phase of development attributed to evolution, and comes into this world prepared to develop its social world. Now development can be arrested at any point that would mean that such an individual would function at the level of development however primitive—or prehuman—a point at which normal development ceased. That is, the brain has not passed through all stages of evolution to the phase of modern man. If normal development occurs he is prepared by a whole past, as it were, for the function of the present. If this is so, viz., that all stages are present in man biologically, it is quite correct to assume it is also a psychological fact. This is supported by revelations from the psyche itself. So when we claim that the beginnings function in the psyche as if man contained within himself an immemorial past, it seems that the structure of the brain itself coincides biologically with such a claim. This would indeed be an interesting study to pursue for anyone with sufficient knowledge of brain structure and psychological phenomena.

Question: It occurs to me that letting the unconscious speak freely is a borderline condition. What would you say about it?

Answer: Yes. That is the important point which must not be overlooked. In a psychotic condition the ego has no say at all. The unconscious takes the place of consciousness. In Active Imagination there is a voluntary submission to unconscious processes, with the ego aware that it is there and able to assert itself again. That is the requirement of the guru or analyst, to see that the tides of the unconscious do not wash the ego away.

Question: Is this why we do not reduce Active Imagination and criticize it as we do dreams? I mean because the ego is involved?

Answer: Thank you for that question. Yes, we do not criticize or reduce a creative process—we try to understand its individual message. We are touching the life-forming force of an individual.

With dreams it is different although we have also to be careful how we handle them—the dream speaks from the "other side" mainly in a compensating way. Active Imagination has to do with the whole person and therefore it has to be handled with understanding and delicacy. The patient, by beginning to discover its connection with archetypal material, with parallels, etc., gets in touch with it in a positive way and learns what has to be learned, which is, of course, so individual that even an analyst cannot and dare not contribute too much in this regard. The main issue is overlooked if one gets caught by the need (which is often personal, anyway) to reduce creative processes to symptoms.

Glossary

Anima and Animus: These are archetypal figures in the unconscious of mankind. They are formed of personal and impersonal inherited elements. They compensate the outer personality. That is, in a man the anima adds feminine characteristics differing from his accepted attitude. In woman the animus adds the masculine to her femininity. The anima adds Eros to a man, and the animus adds discrimination to a woman. These images are formed in a man by the inherited or collective picture of woman and also by his experience of woman in outer reality, the mother, etc. In woman it is inherited ideas, collective ideas, personal experience, the father, etc. Thus they belong to the inner world and are powerful archetypes which can govern every nuance of life. In depth psychology they are made conscious and their autonomous power lessened. In a man the anima may be first recognized in moods foreign to his conscious masculine attitudes. In woman they might appear as arbitrary opinions that are not in line with her real feminine feeling. Being made up of both conscious and unconscious, they are the bridge to unconscious contents. They can move out of an autonomous, often negative, role to support the wholeness of the personality.

Archetype: Archetypes are psychic organs common to mankind. They are inherited patterns or possibilities. They are the sleeping dominants of the unconscious. Archetypes are not filled out with personal memory images but go beyond into ancestral inheritance. They belong to the image of the world it has taken aeons to form, so certain "ways" become instinctive. Therefore instincts are archetypes, patterns of the unconscious. Archetypes are not knowable in themselves but can be inferred from images and behavior such autonomous patterns produce.

Archetypal Image: The image emerging from the unconscious which points to a certain archetype not knowable in itself but discerned, for the archetype itself rooted in the beginnings is beyond comprehension. Successive generations of experience can alter the image which still speaks of primordial factors. Beyond certain ancestral patterns are the universal patterns. Here we find the more universal mythological images, archaic images, etc.

Chthonic: Of the earth, earth spirit, lower world. (Mythology: Zeus stands outside the world as supreme power, Chronos denotes time, and Chthonia represents primitive matter or earth spirit.)

Consciousness: This contains attitudes with which a person faces his immediate external environment. Through consciousness he rationalizes, analyzes, and it gives him a basis of behavior.

Collective Unconscious or Objective Psyche: Psychic area greater-than-individual. It refers not to what could have been conscious but to what is beyond consciousness, hence essentially unconscious. A preconscious structure existing prior to unity of personality. Archetypes are contained in the objective psyche. Hence man inherits patterns or tendencies. This does not mean that man inherits ideas but that he inherits idea-forming tendencies which manifest as archetypal images. From this area the myth-formulating images appear. Such motifs are not inherited ideas but emerge as expressions of psychic processes.

Ego: The ego is a "complex of representations" or a complex of consciousness patterns by inner and outer tendencies and experiences. The ego is not the total psyche, the greater part of which is unconscious, but is the center of the field of consciousness. The ego always contains something of the collective in which it exists as well as personal traits. The ego has that which is common to all egos and at the same time exercises a certain amount of free will. The first step in ego formation is to discriminate oneself from objects; a process of stabilizing and concretizing. Thus the ego is purposeful. This complex unity makes it possible for the ego to know how it feels, etc. Its strength is discernment while a weak ego is near to original unconsciousness. Jung discriminates between the ego and the self as understood in Analytical Psychology. The self actually includes the ego as well as the unconscious psyche. The ego has the strange position of being as much a content as a condition of consciousness.[1]

Functions of Consciousness: There are four functions of consciousness: thinking, feeling, intuition, and sensation. Only one function is as a rule superior, two auxiliary, the fourth inferior. E.g., if intuition is the function by which one adjusts, then sensation or the reality function is weak. If thinking is first it follows feeling is weak, and so on. The idea of four functions is more than schematic. Observation of different ways of behaving and approaching the situation gave Jung his first insight into functional differences in orientation. Intuition and sensation are irrational functions. Thinking and feeling are rational functions.

Function, Transcendent: This is the function which unifies; includes in itself all functions. Known as fifth or transcendent function.

Libido: Psychic energy. Life drive. The dynamic life drive is made of pairs of opposites; when opposites flow together they fulfill their purpose. When one of a pair is overcharged its opposite suffers loss, hence a psychic unbalance.

Myth: The expression of archetypal imagery. It is an impersonal expression of archetypal powers.

Opposites: Progression, regression.

Personal Unconscious or Shadow: Things forgotten or repressed. Personal fantasies and dreams. Peripheral material not ready for consciousness. More or less can be equated with Freud's Unconscious Repressed.

Persona: The persona is a mask built up (education and other factors) as a front presented to the world. Mr. So-and-So appears before his public in a certain recognizable way which can differ from the ego. Life demands certain adaptation and so the persona is built to accommodate movement into the collective.

[1] C. G. Jung, *Psychological Types*, page 540.

It is the outer rather than the real personality. Identification
with the persona means loss of persona which casts the shadow
which is a compensating aspect of the personality. Neither ego
nor shadow is identical with the psyche, which is a totality of
psychic contents; they are complexes within the total psyche.

Psychic Energy: Energy operating in the psyche; a concept used
as a comparative basis for measurement of energic forces. While
such a concept cannot be defined it can be measured in terms
of individual manifestations.

Principle of Opposites: This principle does not postulate a concept of the nature of being but rather a way of thinking about
psychic phenomena as they appear. Life energy depends on
forces held in opposition. Such opposites flow together, unless
obstructed in reciprocal action.

Self: The psychological definition for the totality of conscious
and unconscious. Since the unconscious has limitless borders,
the self is a symbolic figure including and transcending consciousness. The widening of the ego through knowledge of the
unconscious is the becoming of a self. The self is a living symbol
designating something that we can experience and know to
exist, even though its borders are unknowable.

Symbol: The symbol expresses things that are partly known and
partly unknowable or beyond comprehension. It imparts meaning beyond rational conceptual expression. E.g., if we see a
man with a winged motif on his uniform we know he is an
aviator. It is a knowable sign and not a symbol. If we see an
icon, say, with a lion, wings, etc., it is a symbol expressing
something beyond rational language. When something cannot
be expressed rationally the symbol conveys a meaning which
is beyond.

Bibliography

APOCRYPHA, The. *Ecclesiasticus.* Cambridge University Press.
BAYLEY, HAROLD. *Lost Language of Symbolism.* Williams & Norgate, 1952.
BAYNES, H. G. *Mythology of the Soul.* Routledge & Kegan Paul, 1954.
BENNET, E. A. C. G. *Jung.* Barrie & Rockliff, 1961.
BLAKE, William.
COPTIC TEXTS. *Gospel According to Thomas.* Translators A. Guillaumon, H.-C. Puech, G. Guispel, W. Till, Yassah 'Abd Al Masih. Collins, London, 1959.
CUMONT, FRANZ. *The Mysteries of Mithra.* Translator Thomas J. McCormack. Kegan Paul Trench Trübner & Co., 1910.
DODD, *Martyrdom of Peter.*
DUNKERLEY, Roderic (Translator). *The Unwritten Gospel.* George Allen & Unwin, 1925.
FLAUBERT, Gustave. *The Temptations of St. Anthony.* Translator René Francis. Duckworth & Co., 1915.
FORDHAM, Michael, *Journal of Analytical Psychology*, May, 1956.
The Objective Psyche. Routledge & Kegan Paul, 1958.
FRANZ, M-L. v. *Archetypal Patterns in Fairy Tales.* Privately circulated.
GUEBER, H. A. *Myths of the Norsemen.* Geo. G. Harrap, 1908.
HANNAH, Barbara. Unpublished Lectures at the C. G. Jung Institute, Zürich.
HARDING, Esther. *Woman's Mysteries.* Pantheon, 1955.
HOMER. *Odyssey.* Translator E. V. Rieu. Penguin, 1953.
JENNER, Mrs. H. *Our Lady in Art.*
JUNG, C. G. *Contributions to Analytical Psychology.* Translators H. G. & Cary Baynes. Kegan Paul, 1945.
Aion. Translator R. F. C. Hull. Routledge & Kegan Paul, 1959.
Answer to Job. Translator R. F. C. Hull, Routledge & Kegan Paul, 1954.
Essays on Contemporary Events. Translators Elizabeth Welsh, Barbara Hannah, Mary Briner. Kegan Paul, 1947.
"The Spirit of Psychology" in *Spirit and Nature* (Papers from the Eranos Yearbooks 1). Routledge & Kegan Paul, 1955.

Mysterium Coniunctionis. Routledge & Kegan Paul, 1963.

Practice of Psychotherapy. Translator R. F. C. Hull, Routledge & Kegan Paul, 1954.

Psychological Types. Translator H. Godwin Baynes. Routledge & Kegan Paul, 1949.

Psychology and Alchemy. Translator R. F. C. Hull. Routledge & Kegan Paul, 1953.

Psychology and Religion: West and East. Translator R. F. C. Hull. Routledge & Kegan Paul, 1958.

Visions. Private Seminars of C. G. Jung at the C. G. Jung Institute, Zürich.

JUNG, C. G., and KERENYI, C. *Introduction to a Science of Mythology*. Translator R. F. C. Hull. Routledge & Kegan Paul, 1951.

JUNG, C. G., and WILHELM, Richard. *Secret of the Golden Flower*. Translator Cary F. Baynes. Routledge & Kegan Paul, 1950.

KERENYI, C., and JUNG, C. G. *Introduction to a Science of Mythology*. Routledge & Kegan Paul, 1951.

KIRSCH, James. *Journey to the Moon*. Studien zür Analytischer Psychologie, C. G. Jung VI. Rascher, Zürich.

Enigma of Moby Dick. Privately circulated.

LAYARD, John. *Incest Tabu and the Virgin Archetype*. Francs-Jahrbuch XII. Rhein Verlag, Zürich, 1945.

MEAD, G. R. S. *Fragments of a Faith Forgotten*. Translator G. R. S. Mead, Chelsea, 1906. Theosophical Publishing Soc. London & Benares.

Thrice Greatest Hermes. Translator G. R. S. Mead. John M. Watkins, London, 1949.

NEUMANN, Erich. *The Great Mother*. Translator Ralph Manheim. Routledge & Kegan Paul, 1955.

Amor and Psyche. Translator Ralph Manheim. Routledge & Kegan Paul, 1956.

OXYRHYNCHUS.

PLOTINUS. *Select Works of Plotinus*. Thomas Taylor. G. Bell & Sons, London, 1929.

RADIN, Paul. *The Trickster*. With Commentaries by C. Kerenyi & C. G. Jung. Routledge & Kegan Paul, 1956.

VULGATE.

WILHELM, Richard, and JUNG, C. G. *Secret of the Golden Flower*. Translator Cary F. Baynes. Routledge & Kegan Paul, 1950.

(See page 173 for Additional Bibliography)

Reference Information

References to the writings of C. G. Jung in *Old Wise Woman* can be found by paragraph number in *The Collected Works of C. G. Jung* published in the United States by Princeton University Press.

Old Wise Woman				*Collected Works*			
Chapter	1,	footnote	4	Volume	10,	paragraph	437
”	1,	”	7	”	8,	”	402
Chapter	2,	footnote	2	Volume	6,	paragraph	712
”	2,	”	3	”	6,	”	713
”	2,	”	4	”	6,	”	837
”	2,	”	5	”	6,	”	720
”	2,	”	6	”	6,	”	720, 721, 722
Chapter	3,	footnote	1	Volume	9ii,	paragraph	333
”	3,	”	4	”	12,	”	359, 360
”	3,	”	6	”	14,	”	333
”	3,	”	8	”	14,	”	226
”	3,	”	11	”	11,	”	575
”	3,	”	12	”	11,	”	646
Chapter	4,	footnote	5	Volume	11,	paragraph	624
”	4,	”	6	”	11,	”	638
”	4,	”	7	”	11,	”	640
”	4,	”	10	”	13,	Part IV	
”	4,	”	11	”	12,	paragraph	518
Chapter	5,	footnote	2	Volume	12,	paragraph	30
Chapter	6,	footnote	4	Volume	11,	paragraph	356
”	6,	”	5	”	11,	”	420
”	6,	”	6	”	12,	”	172
”	6,	”	7	”	12,	”	173
”	6,	”	9	”	6,	”	311

Chapter	7, footnote	1	Volume	11, paragraph	390

Chapter	8, footnote	3	Volume	9ii, paragraph	343

Chapter	9, footnote	1	Volume	9ii, paragraph	338
”	9, ”	4	”	12, ”	192
”	9, ”	17	”	16, ”	456

Chapter	10, footnote	7	Volume	11, paragraph	757
”	10, ”	9	”	11, ”	167

Chapter	12, footnote	5	Volume	6, paragraph	310
”	12, ”	6	”	12, ”	13
”	12, ”	7	”	12, ”	19

Glossary, footnote 1			Volume	6, paragraph	706

Additional Bibliography

BAYNES, H. G. *Mythology of the Soul.* London: Rider & Co., 1969.
BENNET, E. A. *C. G. Jung.* New York: E. P. Dutton & Co., 1962.
CUMONT, Franz. *Mysteries of Mithra.* Translated by Thomas J. Mc-
Cormack. New York: Dover Publications, 1911.
FLAUBERT, Gustave. *Tentation De Saint-Antoine.* New York: French
& European Publications, 1954.
FRANZ, Marie-Louise von. *Interpretation of Fairytales.* New York:
Spring Publications, 1970.
HARDING, Esther. *Woman's Mysteries.* New York: C. G. Jung Founda-
tion for Analytical Psychology Publication, 1971.
JUNG, C. G. *The Collected Works of C. G. Jung.* Princeton: Prince-
ton University Press, Bollingen Series XX. Editors: Sir Herbert
Read, Michael Fordham, M.D., M.R.C.P., Gerhard Adler, Ph.D.
and William McGuire, Exec. Ed., Translated by R. F. C. Hull.
    Volume 1. Psychiatric Studies. 1970.
    "   2. Experimental Researches, 1973.
    "   3. The Psychogenesis of Mental Disease. 1960.
    "   4. Freud and Psychoanalysis. 1961.
    "   5. Symbols of Transformation. 1967.
    "   6. Psychological Types. 1971.
    "   7. Two Essays on Analytical Psychology. 1966.
    "   8. The Structure and Dynamics of the
                  Psyche. 1969.
    "   9. Part 1. The Archetypes and the Collective
                  Unconscious. 1968.
    "   9. Part 2. Aion. 1968.
    "   10. Civilization in Transition. 1970.
    "   11. Psychology and Religion: West and East. 1969.
    "   12. Psychology and Alchemy. 1968.
    "   13. Alchemical Studies. 1968.
    "   14. Mysterium Coniunctionis. 1970.
    "   15. The Spirit in Man, Art, and Literature. 1966.
    "   16. The Practice of Psychotherapy. 1966.
    "   17. The Development of Personality. 1954.
————. *Interpretations of Visions: Excerpts from the Notes of Mary
Foote.* New York: Spring Publications, 10 Installments, 1960-69.

JUNG, C. G., and KERÉNYI, C. *Essays on a Science of Mythology: The Myth of the Divine Child and the Mysteries of Eleusis.* Translated by R. F. C. Hull. Princeton: Princeton University Press, Bollingen Series, 1969.

NEUMANN, Erich. *The Great Mother: An Analysis of the Archetype.* Translated by Ralph Manheim. Princeton: Princeton University Press, Bollingen Series, 1963.

———. *Amor and Psyche: The Psychic Development of the Feminine.* Translated by Ralph Manheim. Princeton: Princeton University Press, Bollingen Series, 1956.

RADIN, Paul. *The Trickster: A Study in American Indian Mythology.* Commentaries by C. G. Jung and C. Kerényi. New York: Schocken Books, 1972.

WILHELM, Richard, and JUNG, C. G. *The Secret of the Golden Flower.* Translated by Cary F. Baynes. New York: Harcourt, Brace & Jovanovich, 1962.

Other C. G. Jung Foundation Books from Shambhala Publications

*Published in association with Daimon Verlag, Einsiedeln, Switzerland.

Snail little "feelers" out of the
Shell, little head, body; silver
lines, paths where She moves
She leaves silver paths.
Her movement is graceful,
gentle, curious, smooth, Slow.
Slow as a snail.
Her Shell Sits her perfectly,
is beautiful, is curved.
Shell of repeating curves,
spiral, rounded soft curves
whole house of one curve
holding her She keeps
her House.